Impeachment of Donald Trump Could be the Third?

Dr. Zulfiquar Ahmed
Associate Professor
Department of Law
Rajshahi University
Rajshahi-6204
Bangladesh
Email: zulfiquarcyberlaw at gmail.com

Copyright © 2019 Dr. Zulfiquar Ahmed

All rights reserved.

ISBN: 9781710268171

DEDICATION

This book is dedicated to

All

The Presidents of the America

Except

Donald J. Trump

TABLE OF CONTENTS

CHAPTER ONE	1
INTRODUCTION TO IMPEACHMENT	1
What is Impeachment?	2
Who May Be Impeached?	6
CHAPTER TWO	9
IMPEACHMENT PROCEDURES	9
How does the impeachment process work?	10
Impeachment Proceedings of the House of Representatives	11
Initiation of Impeachment	12
Investigation of Impeachment	14
House of Representative Action after Receiving the Committee Report	16
Notification by the House and Senate Response	17
The Senate: Sole Power to Try Impeachments	18
Trial Preparation in the Senate	20
Trial Procedure in the Senate	21
Judgment of the Senate	27
Judicial Review in Impeachment Question	29
Pathway of Impeachment Process of Donald Trump	32
Pathway of the House of Representatives	32
Pathway of the Senate	40

CHAPTER THREE	42
IMPEACHABLE OFFENSES	42
What are impeachable offenses?	43
CHAPTER FOUR	67
PREVIOUS IMPEACHMENT FACTS	67
Previous impeachment investigations and results	68
CHAPTER FIVE	81
Grounds for Impeachment of Donald Trump	81
General Grounds for Impeachment of Donald Trump	82
Donald Trump's Impeachable Offenses	84
Possible Articles of Impeachment against Donald Trump	130
CHAPTER SIX	187
Trump Impeachment: Possibility-impossibility	187
Is it really possible to overthrow President Trump?	188
Can Trump Be Acquitted from the Impeachment prosecution?	192

PREFACE

The debate over the United States 45th President *Donald J. Trump* is not new. His words and activities are nothing out of it. His statement is a regular issue in the talk of the town. The President *Donald J. Trump* is now at the center of attention of the world politics.

This Book has been arranged as a reference book for the researchers of Law, Government & Politics, Public Administration, Sociology, and Political Science. The book will also be useful for students, teachers, politicians, House Members, Senators, Judges, Juries, Attorneys, social workers, and legal experts.

America is related with the norms and values of democracy, the values of liberty, the independent of freedom, the esteem of rule of the law, the dignity of the human, the origin, the color, the religion, the gender, the sexual conduct or the freedom of political view. But the President *Donald J. Trump*'s vanity, self-admiration, self-absorption, self-obsession, conceit, smugness, superiority, arrogance, self-centeredness, self-regard, egotism, shamelessness, magical thinking, envy, exploitation, abuse, manipulation, mistreatment, and egoism has thrown America into existential threat. His abusive comments and actions towards marginalized groups, specially - Muslims, Mexicans, women, and disable people, have spoiled original identity of the America and endangered the high standard of the America in the world as well as the system of tying in a yarn of the West to the East has endangered by the President *Donald J. Trump*. He also shows speedily unstable and narrow expressions of emotions, feelings and sentiments and his conduct and behavior is over-reactive and forcefully expressed.

Trump announced his nomination on June 9, 2015 under the Republican Party in the presidential election. Trump has been able to gain media attention and public support through his previous campaign activities. In the elections held on November 7, 2016 he received 306 electoral votes and was elected president.

The United States 45th President *Donald J. Trump*'s political complexity is not diminishing. Several times it seemed that *Donald J. Trump* was facing impeachment in Congress. In the end, he had to face impeachment investigation.

Now, the present debate on impeachment investigation is Trump's phone call with the Ukrainian president. Nancy Pelosi, speaker of the House of Representatives, has recently ordered a formal investigation. The process of impeachment against him has begun in Congress.

If *Donald Trump* is removed from the impeachment, then Vice President Mike Pence will automatically be replaced. He will fulfill the current term of the President, which will end on January 20, 2021.

It is said that the announcement of the

impeachment in the Congress is deeply divided the United States only one year left before the election. The effect of impeachment investigation is far-reaching.

While everyone's attention is drawn to US impeachment, this is not a rare occurrence in world politics. **Robert Mugabe**, the recently deceased Zimbabwean president, faced impeachment on November 2017 after 37 years in power.

The impeachment process against the 36th President of Brazil **Dilma Vana Rousseff** began on May 2o16. She was ousted in the Senate by 61-20 votes and removal from office on 31 August 2016.

My dear readers, read this book ***"Impeachment of Donald Trump: Could be the Third?"*** in a breath and find out why the US President *Donald Trump* needs to be impeached and how the impeachment prosecution process goes on, and how complicated and difficult the procedure of impeachment is, and whether he can be impeached at all as well as find out the difficulties and niceties of the event.

Dr. Zulfiquar Ahmed
November, 2019
Rajshahi University

CHAPTER ONE
INTRODUCTION TO IMPEACHMENT

What is Impeachment?

Impeachment is the process of accusing a person in the highest officer of the state or Federal government. It can also be called a removal process of the civil officers. The impeachment may come under the presidency of the country, the Prime Minister, the judges of the Supreme Court and the honorable persons.

In general, the word *'impeachment'* means accusation, allegation, suspicion, complaint, charge, indictment, and prosecution namely accusing the head of state. The impeachment is called for removal of any allegation of incompetence, disability or any other anti-public interest in the Parliament or Special Tribunal against the Head of State or any civil officer.

The origin of impeachment is dated to ancient Athens. Its adopted in the U.S. Constitution was secured by the inspiration of English Common Law on the Framers of the U.S. Constitution. So, a procedure that is used to charge, try, and remove public officials for delinquency while in office. It is an ultimate constitutional authority belonging to the Congress.

To protect the balance of power, the US drafters of the constitution have added a clause of impeachments to the constitution, whereby

Congress can remove the president in the case of an unjust incident. In 1787, there was a constitutional convention held in Philadelphia. At the end of fervid debate, the delegates agreed that the president could be removed for *'treason, bribery, or other high Crimes and Misdemeanors'*.

The process of impeachment must begin with the United States House of Representatives. It is a part of the US Congress.

Impeachment is a double-edged weapon. Though it was considered to check oppressor, tyrant, or extortioner, Thomas Jefferson also termed as impeachment *"the most formidable weapon for the purpose of a dominant faction that was ever contrived."*[1] Impeachment is a constitutional process under which an elected official and civil official, including the president, vice-president, is accused with a crime or offenses demanding elimination from office. Unlike other elected government officials, who can be accused with offenses and removed from office if convicted in a court, president, vice-president or other civil officers cannot be accused with a criminal offense under present Department of Criminal Justice system.

Impeachment has served as a very significant

---

[1] Jon Meacham, et.al., *Impeachment: An American History,* Thorndike Press, 2018.

instrument in the United States. It assists as a basic suggestion to the government officials that the individuals will consider the government officials in question responsible for activities that conflict with the eventual benefits of the country—defilement, improper utilization of the financial matter, in any event, for cases that conflict with society's ethics and rules, as found in the United States.

So, it is called that impeachment is a constitutional therapy routed to genuine offenses against the arrangement of government. It is the initial phase in a remedial procedure—that of expulsion from government office and conceivable preclusion from holding further office. The reason for impeachment authorized in the U.S. constitution isn't close to physical punishment; rather, its purpose is principally to uphold and keep up constitutional government. The object for impeachment under the Constitution is also demonstrated by the limited extent of the remedy (expulsion from office and conceivable exclusion from future office) and by the expressed grounds for impeachment (treason, bribery, and other high crimes and misdemeanors). It isn't limited whether treason and bribery are criminal. Ever more significant, they are constitutional wrongs that destabilize the organization of government, or subvert the respectability of office and even the Constitution itself, and hence are "high" offenses as in word was utilized in English impeachments.

Therefore, the term *'impeach'* is utilized in various ways at different phases of the judicial procedures. A Member ascends on the floor to 'impeach' an official in displaying a resolution or memorial or remembrance. The House of representative polls to 'impeach' in the constitutional sense when it receives an impeachment resolution furthermore, going with articles. Then, the Senate at that point directs a trial on these articles and either convicts by 66% vote or vindicates the 'impeached' alleged federal government official.

Lastly, it is crystal clear that an impeachment is introduced by a written accusation, called the *"Articles of Impeachment,"* which prescribes the offense accused. This impeachment power is described by the U.S. Constitution. The House of representative is specified the *"sole Power of Impeachment"* under Article 1 § 2 of the U.S. Constitution and the Senate is specified *"the sole Power to try all Impeachments"* under Article 1 § 3. Impeachment refers to proceedings brought against certain federal public officials for offenses, abuse of office, or other misconduct while the official holds public office.[2]

In order to start the process of impeachment there must be a resolution passed in the general majority. If a resolution passed, the next step will be to hold a Senate trial, which is the second part of Congress. Here the senators will act as judges or juries. They will decide whether the president is impeached as a guilty or innocent. And two-thirds of the senators will have to vote for impeachment if the president is removed.

Impeachment or impeachment procedure is very rare in case of president in the American history. Impeachment or impeachment procedure preserves the balance of power of the president. The United States Congress, where laws are enacted, can face top officials, including the country's president.

The United States Constitution states that the president may be removed from his position, meaning that he may be impeached for certain crimes. These offenses include: treason, bribery or any other major or minor offense[3].

Who May Be Impeached?

According to Article II § 4 of the United States' Constitution, the *"President, Vice President, and all civil Officers of the United States"* are the main issue to removal from their office under the

---

[2] David L Hudson, the Handy Law Answer Book, Visible Ink Press, 2010, p. 32.

[3] Any other major or minor offense other is indicated in the U.S. Constitution as 'high Crimes and Misdemeanors'.

impeachment section of the Constitution. The phrase used in the U.S. Constitution are included *"all civil officers of the United States"* denotes to *"those appointed by the President"* under the American national government, whether their duties are administrative, executive or judicial, in the highest or the lowest departments; of the government. But "all civil officers of the United States" phrase used in the U.S. Constitution are not included the officers of the army and navy. And it is also included *"broad enough to include all [those] who hold their appointment from the Federal government."*[4] For this reason, a Member of Congress and a senator of the United States is not a *"civil Officer,"*[5] within the meaning of this clause in the constitution, the Senate overlooked the impeachment of Senator William Blount of Tennessee in 1799, dismissing him instead.[6]

In 1787, when the Constitution's makers met in Philadelphia they seem suitable impeachment clause into a structure that detached

---

[4] Brown, W., *House Practice: A Guide to the Rules, Precedents, and Procedures of the House* ch. 27 §1 (2011) at 604.[hereinafter *House Practice]*

[5] Cong. Research Serv., Library of Cong., 112th Cong., The Constitution of the United States of America: Analysis and Interpretation, Doc. No. 112–9, at 646 (2013) ("all the debate was in terms of the President"), https://www.congress.gov/constitution-annotated/.

[6] Id.

governmental authority into three branches (legislative, executive or judicial), with checks and balances among them.[7] The drafters in Philadelphia took into account impeachment to be a technique for Congress to check the American President. So, this clause in the American Constitution is *"focus[ed] principally on [impeachment's] applicability to the President."*[8] During the constitutional convention, James Madison argued that impeachment is *"indispensable…for defending the Community [against] the incapacity, negligence or perfidy of the [President]."*[9]

The contention that a private citizen who has held no public office may also not be impeached within the meaning of the impeachment provisions of the Constitution.

The contention of the constitutional provision that who was not a civil officer within the meaning of the impeachment provisions of the Constitution was continued by the Senate in 1799. But the federal judges are considered as *"civil officer"* subject to removal under the impeachment provisions of the Constitution.

---

[7] Jared P. Cole et al., Impeachment and Removal, Congressional Research Service, CRS Report for Members and Committees of Congress, No. R44260 (Oct. 29, 2015), p. 1.

[8] Cong. Research Serv. at 650.

[9] Impeachment of the Executive, [20 July] 1787, Founders Online, National Archives; https://founders.archives.gov

CHAPTER TWO
IMPEACHMENT PROCEDURES

How does the impeachment process work?

The term "impeachment" is used in the United States' Constitution for the elimination of a federal government official from his/her office. Although the term "impeachment" is not defined in the United States' Constitution but the impeachment process and procedure is designed in the Constitution very well. This provision needs two distinct proceedings carried out by the separate houses of Congress i.e., the House of Representative and the Senate. The House of Representative officially accepts accusations of misconduct amounting to an impeachable offense, recognized as articles of impeachment by a simple majority of the House. Then the articles of impeachment are progressed to the Senate where the second proceeding occurs: an impeachment trial. The Senate may be removed the accused federal civil officers by vote of a two-thirds majority and also declared disqualified from holding future office.

The United States' Constitution expresses the common principles which regulate the procedural features of impeachment, conferring the authority to impeach in the House of Representatives, while invigorating the Senate with the power to try impeachments. Both the

Senate and the House have planned impeachment procedures to implement these common rules in dealing with a extensive range of impeachment questions.

This chapter delivers a brief overview of the impeachment procedure, reflecting the roles of both the House of Representatives and the Senate during the course of an impeachment investigation and trial.

Impeachment Proceedings of the House of Representatives

The U.S. Constitution provides the *"sole Power of Impeachment"* to the House of Representatives under Article I, § 2, Cl. 5. The House of Representatives follows certain unwritten rules for impeachment proceedings, such as Initiation, Investigation, House Action Subsequent to Receipt of Committee Report and Notification by the House and Senate Response etc.

But the impeachment process in the House of Representatives mostly proceeds in the following three stages by the opinion of Congressional Research Service[10], such as,

---

[10] Congressional Research Service, "The Impeachment Process in the House of Representatives", Under the U.S. Constitution, the House of Representatives, October 10, 2019 https://crsreports.congress.gov

(1) Initiation of the impeachment process;

(2) Judiciary Committee investigation, hearings, and markup of articles of impeachment; and

(3) Full House consideration of the articles of impeachment.

Initiation of Impeachment

Impeachment proceedings inaugurate with the presentation of allegations or charges or accusations, which usually happen when a Member of the House of Representatives presents a resolution or a memorial, or a resolution to empower an impeachment investigation. So, impeachment procedure may be inaugurated in the House of Representatives by a Member of the House of Representatives announcing a charge of impeachment on his or her own initiative.

An impeachment memorial or resolution is similar to a criminal charge by a grand jury. It is a list of unverified allegations that a federal government official has affianced in actions that permit his impeachment. On the other side, the impeachment procedure may be activated by non-Members of the House of Representatives. No extraordinary events control when such a memorial can be presented, although traditionally they have been presented reasonably infrequently. But impeachment really happens when the House, by a simple majority, approves such a resolution.

The Speaker of the House of Representatives must then schedule a time to ponder the memorial or resolution within two legislative days without providing the notice to the majority and the minority House leader. The full House of Representatives could dispose of an impeachment resolution upraised in this approach in any number of ways, including by referring it to the Judiciary Committee instead of by voting on the resolution directly. The House of Representatives could also settle to a motion to bench the resolution and thereby put through of it forever and adversely.

In general, while the House Judiciary Committee operates impeachment investigations, such articles of impeachment have rarely been conferred to other investigation committees. Furthermore, an impeachment investigation may be referred by the House of Representatives through the House Judiciary Committee to one of its subcommittees or to a particularly formed subcommittee for investigation.

All impeachment matters to reach the Senate since 1900 have been grounded on Judiciary

Committee memorials or resolutions. Before the creation of the House Judiciary Committee in 1813, impeachments were referred to a special committee for investigation.

Investigation of Impeachment

In all earlier impeachment procedures, the House of Representative has analyzed the charges before arranging any vote. Typically a preliminary investigation is led by the Judiciary Committee, to which investigating and announcing obligations are appointed by goals after charges have been exhibited. In any case, it is plausible that this examination for investigation and inquiry could be completed by a select commission or special committee. Whenever approved by the House of Representative, the Judiciary Committee may assign a subcommittee or team to explore whether an individual ought to be impeached. For instance, in 2009, the House of Representative passed a resolution approving the Judiciary Committee or an assigned subcommittee or team to investigate whether Judge Porteous ought to be impeached. The resolution additionally approved the taking of statements, the issuance of summons, the payment of funds, and the contracting of staff.

In the last presidential impeachment, a correspondence from the Independent Counsel to the exploring President Bill Clinton was eluded to the Committee on the Judiciary in accordance with a unique resolution announced by the Rules Committee.[11] The resolution likewise guided the Judiciary Committee to analysis the data of information from the Independent Counsel *"to decide whether adequate grounds exist for prescribing the House that a impeachment investigation be started."* The House of Representative, for this situation, later revealed a resolution reported by the Judiciary Committee to empower an inquiry by the council investigation committee.[12]

The focal point of the impeachment investigation is to decide if the individual involved has betrothed in treason, bribery, or other high crimes and misdemeanors. If a sub-committee or team is accused of investigating enquiry a potential impeachment, the Members

---

[11] H.Res.525, 105th Congress. The resolution was privileged for consideration under House Rule XIII, clause 5(a)(4). See also H.Rept. 105-703. The independent counsel had been appointed pursuant to the Ethics in Government Act of 1978. The original law provided that the authority to appoint an independent counsel would expire after five years. The provisions were reauthorized in 1983, 1987, and 1994 but were allowed to expire in 1999. For more information, see archived CRS Report RL30092, *Independent Counsel Statute: Considerations in the Decision on Reauthorization*, by Jack Maskell (available to congressional clients from the author).

[12] H.Res. 581, 105th Congress. *"Authorizing the Committee on the Judiciary to Investigate Whether Sufficient Grounds Exist for the Impeachment of William Jefferson Clinton, President of the United States,"* Congressional Record, daily edition (October 8, 1998), pp. H10015-H10032.

can cast a ballot to prescribe articles of impeachment to the full committee. If the full board of committee, by majority vote, discovers that justification for impeachment exist, a resolution impeaching the person being referred to and presenting explicit claims of wrongdoing or offense, in at least one articles of impeachment, will be accounted for to the full House.

In short, any matter connected to the behavior of any federal government official may arrive at the House of representative and be referred to committee preceding the reception of a resolution guiding a committee to manage an investigation and inquiry. Generally, this has involved petitions and materials from any people of America. Furthermore, standing committees, under their overall investigatory power, can look for data and research charges against officials preceding the endorsement of a resolution to approve an impeachment investigation of inquiry.

House of Representative Action after Receiving the Committee Report

At the end of dialogue and debate, the House of Representative of the USA may ponder about the resolution in general, or may cast vote on each article of impeachment in a different way. Furthermore, similar to the standard practical perspective, the committee's suggestions on article of impeachment as stated in a report in the resolution are no method for authoritative on the House of Representatives. The House of Representatives may cast a ballot to impeach regardless of whether the House Judiciary Committee doesn't prescribe impeachment. In accordance with Article I of the American Constitution, a poll to impeach by the House of Representative of the USA needs a common majority of those present members of the House and voting members of the House by fulfillment of quorum necessities. If the House the House of Representative of the USA votes to impeach, supervisors are then chosen to introduce the issue to the Senate. In modern practice, supervisors have been selected by resolution, even though they generally have been chosen or selected by the Speaker of the House in accordance with a resolution giving such authority upon him.

Notification by the House and Senate Response

The nineteenth century impeachment trial standards procedures apparently need a sequence of activities by the Senate upon the receipt of articles of impeachment from the House of Representatives. The Senate, notwithstanding, much the same as the House of Representatives, can put aside its guidelines by, for instance, consenting to a general resolution. The House of Representatives will likewise accept a resolution so as to inform the Senate of its activity. The Senate, in the wake of accepting such notice, will then accept an instruction advising the House of Representatives that it is prepared to get the managers. In this way, the selected managers will show up before the bar of the Senate to impeach the individual in question and display the articles of impeachment against that accused person. After this method, the managers would back and provide an oral report to the House of Representatives.

The Senate: Sole Power to Try Impeachments

Article I, Section 3, Clause 6 of the US Constitution states that

> *"The Senate shall have the sole Power to try all Impeachments. When sitting for that Purpose, they shall be on Oath or Affirmation. When the President of the United States is tried, the Chief Justice shall preside: And no Person shall be convicted without the Concurrence of two thirds of the Members present."*

The basic authorities, strategies and procedures for Senate impeachment trials are stated in this provision of the US Constitution.

The Framers of the US Constitution conferred the Senate with the *"sole Power to try Impeachments"* for a few causes.

Firstly, the Framers of the US Constitution are very trustworthy because Senators would be better educated, more righteous, higher-minded, more decent and morally honest than Members of the House of Representatives and accordingly outstandingly ready to choose skillfully the most troublesome of political inquiries.

Secondly, the Framers of the US Constitution conferred the Senate instead of the judiciary or any legal authority or tribunals with the power to try impeachments since they supported, as Alexander Hamilton clarified in The Federalist No. 65, a *"numerous court for the trial of impeachments."* He assumed such a authority would be appropriate to deal with the procedural weights of an impeachment trial, in which it, in contrast to the judiciary or any legal authority or tribunals or judges, should

> *"never be tied down by such strict rules, either in the delineation of the offense by the prosecutor, or in the construction of it by judges, as in the common cases serve to limit the discretion of courts in favor of personal security."*

Additionally, Hamilton clarified that

> *"[t]he awful discretion which a court of*

impeachments must necessarily have to doom to honor or infamy the most confidential and the most distinguished characters of the community forbids the commitment of the trust to a small number of persons."

Trial Preparation in the Senate

Impeachment procedures in the Senate are administered now by the Rules of Procedure and Practice in the Senate when Sitting on Impeachment Trials.[13] After presenting of introducing of the articles of impeachment and association of the Senate to think about the considering the impeachment, the Senate will give a writ of request or subpoena to the respondent, notifying the accused person in question regarding the date on which appearance and answer ought to be made. On the date set up by the Senate, the respondent may attend physically or by counsel. The accused may also decide not to attend before the authority. In the subsequent occasion, the procedures progress as if a *"not liable"* or *"not guilty"* plea were arrived. The respondent may challenge, contending that the individual in question is certifiably not a civil official subject to impeachment, or that the charges recorded don't comprise adequate reason

---

[13] "Rules of Procedure and Practice in the Senate when Sitting on Impeachment Trials," Senate Manual, S. Doc. 113-1, §§170-95, at 223-231

for impeachment. On the other hand, the respondent may also answer the articles of impeachment conveyed against the person individually. The House of Representatives has customarily recorded duplication to the respondent's answer, and the pleadings may proceed with a rejoinder, surrejoinder, and similiter.

Trial Procedure in the Senate

According to VI *Cannon's Precedents of the House of Representatives* §§ 508, when pleadings have closed, the Senate will fixed a date for trial. Upon setting up this date, the Senate will make an instruction the managers of the House of Representatives or their counsel to provide the Sergeant at Arms of the Senate with data material in regards to witnesses who are to be summoned, and will additional specify that more witnesses might be summoned by application to the Presiding Officer. Under Article I, Section 3, proviso 6 of the US Constitution, the Chief Justice presides over the Senate impeachment trial if the President is being tried for impeachment.

There are three specific necessities for impeachment trials. Firstly, the necessity is that Senators be on Oath or Affirmation in impeachment trials was clearly intended to put forth for them the very extreme sincerity of the event. Secondly, the prerequisite for the Chief Justice to direct presidential impeachment trials emphasizes the weightiness and significance of the event and means to stay away from the conceivable conflict of interest of a Vice President's presiding over the procedure for the expulsion of the one authority remaining among him and the presidency. Furthermore, the last super major prerequisite was intended to encourage thoughtful discussion and to make elimination probable just through a consensus that differs over dissenting separations. This present necessity's effect is clear in the way that the Senate has convicted seven of sixteen individuals impeached by the House of Representatives. It was contributory in Andrew Johnson's trial, as the majority fell one vote short of expelling him from government office. In President William Jefferson Clinton's trial, there was never an issue of his removal so long as all of the forty-five Democrats in the Senate uniformly opposed his removal.

Notwithstanding the prerequisites in the Constitution's content, three remarkable queries have emerged about Senate power to attempt impeachments. The Senate must do once the House of Representatives impeaches somebody; this is the first minimum requirement. After the

House's first prosecution, this query appeared in 1797. One day after the House of Representatives impeached Senator William Blount, the Senate ousted him by a vote of 25–1. Blount appealed the Senate needed position to try impeachment to him since Senators were not impeachable and, in any occasion, he never again engaged an office from which he could be impeached. The Senate arranged a vote to discharge the impeachment resolution against the ousted Blount for absence of authority. Henceforward, numerous Senators have understood this vote as supporting their position to reject an impeachment without a full-scale trial.

The second query is the scope of the Chief Justice's authoritative position as presiding officer to purify unilateral rulings verdicts. Chief Justice Salmon Chase assured the position to choose certain procedural queries all alone in the first presidential impeachment trial in 1868, then the Senate confronted numerous of his decisions and overruled him at least twice. But, in President Clinton's impeachment trial in 1999, Chief Justice William H. Rehnquist make rulings on some procedural questions, no Senator challenged, no question of overruled in any of these decisions.

A third question rotates around which

techniques of proceedings the Senate must utilize in impeachment trials. Since the Constitution both furnishes the Senate with the *"sole power to try impeachments"* and enables *"[e]ach House...to determine the Rules of its Proceedings,"* the Senate has planned its particular impeachment trial systems (first recorded by Thomas Jefferson when he was Vice President). In President Johnson's impeachment trial, the Senate detailed an extra set of rules that have to a great extent stayed unblemished from that point forward and were trailed by the Senate in President Clinton's impeachment trial.

In 1936, the Senate changed these principles to incorporate Rule XI, which permits the appointment of few Senators to work as a trial committee to assemble proof and take witness. The Senate has utilized trial committees on just three events during the 1980s to help with fact-finding in regards to impeachment articles endorsed by the House of Representatives against three federal district judges. Prior to the Senate and in federal court, all three judges confronted the authenticity of trial committees. They contended the Senate's *"power to try impeachments"* forced on the full Senate the commitment to direct a full trial. The Senate opposed that it had total authority over how to design procedures and that Senators' political responsibility was the main check on this power. At last, the Supreme Court acknowledged the Senate's contentions in Nixon vs. United States (1993) on the main ground that the Senate's authority to try impeachments incorporated the non-reviewable ultimate option to decide how to lead its trials. The Court didn't address the legitimacy of judicial review of the Senate's conceivable unorthodoxy from any unequivocal defend essential by the United States Constitution for impeachment trials.

The Senate established some other procedural queries brought up in the 1980s, comprising with the relevance and pertinence of the Fifth Amendment Due Process Clause to and the essential guidelines of proof and burden of proof for impeachment trials. The Senate decided that receiving a uniform principle on these queries was illogical on the grounds that it came up short on the methods for upholding any such rule against Senators. It settled down that each question was an issue for the Senators to choose for themselves.

In impeachment trials, the full Senate may get proof and take verification of the evidence, or may command the Presiding Officer to employ a committee of Senators to fill this need. [14] In the

---

[14] Senate Manual: Impeachment Rules, Rule XI.

last alternative is utilized, the committee will show a certified transcript of the procedures to the full body of Senate. The Senate will decide investigations of competency, pertinence, and materiality[15]. The Senate may also take more testimony in an open Senate, or may arrange that the whole trial be before the full Senate. [16]

At the commencement of the trial, House managers and advice for the respondent submit and present initial contentions delineation the charges to be set up and contradicted. The managers and supervisors for the House of Representatives present their first argument and legal reasoning. During the sequence of the trial various evidence and proof is displayed and witnesses may be analyzed, examined and cross-examined.

The Senate has not accepted any standard principles of proof and evidence to be utilized during an impeachment trial. The Presiding Officer owns special power to decide on all evidentiary issues. Moreover, the Presiding Officer may place any such question to a vote before the Senate. However, any Senator may demand that a conventional vote be taken on a specific question. Final contentions in the trial

---

[15] Id.
[16] Id.

will be introduced by each side, with the managers for the House of Representatives introductory and concluding.

Judgment of the Senate

At this time, when the demonstration and presentation of proof, evidence and argument-contention by the managers and counsel for the respondent has finished up, the Senate generally meets in closed-door meeting to deliberate. Voting on whether to condemn on the articles of impeachment initiates upon come back to open session, with yeas and nays being counted as to each article separately. An impeachment conviction on an article of impeachment necessitates a two-thirds vote of those Senators present in the Senate. If the respondent is sentenced on at least one or more of the articles impeachment against that person, the Presiding Officer will articulate the judgment of conviction and expulsion. No conventional vote is required for expulsion, as it is an essential impact of the conviction.199 The Senate has not generally decided on each article of impeachment before it; for instance, when the Senate didn't convict President Andrew Johnson in the decisions on three of the articles of impeachment against him, the Senate didn't decide on the remaining articles impeachment.

The Senate may afterwards decide on whether the impeached official will be prohibited for ineligibility from again holding an office of public belief and trust under the United States. If this choice is followed, a straightforward majority vote is necessary.

The Constitution attaches the obligation of attempting impeachments upon the Senate. However a few Senators have questioned whether they have the necessary ability to attempt impeachments. Rule XI was received as a reaction to poor participation and arrangement by Senators in impeachment trials in the mid twentieth century. However even during the 1980s, a few Senators asserted that they had not tried to get ready before casting a ballot, and such procedures occupied their verves from legislative function of more prominent worry to their constituents. Others contended the procedures reestablished their trust in the Senate's institutional fitness to direct them. In any occasion, the Framers of the United States Constitution conferred that duty in the Senate and no place else.

The last question is the ongoing debate over how viable impeachment is as a solution for executive or judicial misconduct by the federal officials. After the discharge of President Clinton, a few analysts have pondered whether impeachment is a significant alternative for managing a prevalent President's delinquency or misconduct. Some think that Clinton's release reinforced the presidency since it makes it fewer probable coming Presidents will confront serious impeachment endeavors for personal delinquency or misconduct. Others believe Clinton's exoneration replicates a suitable compromise that was reliable with the systematic arrangement: he had been impeached by the House of Representatives and hence humiliated for his misbehavior but not removed from office. Approval of these contending perspectives must anticipate future prosecution preliminaries.

Judicial Review in Impeachment Question

It was long time supposed that no judicial review of the impeachment procedure was conceivable, that impeachment displays a genuine "*political question*" case, i. e. , that the Constitution's delivery on the Senate of the "*sole*" authority to try impeachments is a literarily obvious constitutional responsibility or promise of trial procedures to the Senate to choose without court evaluation. That hypothesis was not challenged until very recently, when Judges Nixon and Hastings confronted their Senate convictions.[17]

Therefore, Impeachment procedures have been tested in federal court on various events.

In the Judge Nixon case, the Court held that a case to judicial review of an issue emerging in an impeachment trial in the Senate introduces a non-justiciable *"political question."*[18] Possibly most meaningfully, the Supreme Court has decided that an assessment to the Senate's utilization of a trial committee to take proof offered a non-justiciable political question.[19]. In particular, the Court dismissed a case that the Senate had left from the importance of the term *"try"* in the impeachment provision by depending on a specific committee to take proof with testimony. In any case, the Court's *"political question"* examination has more extensive application, and seems to put the entire impeachment procedure

---

[17] Both judges challenged the use under Rule XI of a trial committee to hear the evidence and report to the full Senate, which would then carry out the trial. The rule was adopted in the aftermath of an embarrassingly sparse attendance at the trial of Judge Louderback in 1935. National Comm. Report, supra at 50–53, 54– 57; Grimes, supra at 1233–37. In the Nixon case, the lower courts held the issue to be non-justiciable (*Nixon v. United States*, 744 F. Supp. 9 (D.D.C. 1990), aff'd, 938 F.2d 239 (D.C. Cir. 1991), but a year later a district court initially ruled in Judge Hastings' favor. Hastings v. United States, 802 F. Supp. 490 (D.D.C. 1992), vacated, 988 F.2d 1280 (D.C. Cir. 1993).
[18] Nixon v. United States, 506 U.S. 224 (1993). Nixon at the time of his conviction and removal from office was a federal district judge in Mississippi.
[19] Id.

beyond reach to judicial review.[20]

In *Nixon v. United States*, the House of Representatives approved articles of impeachment against the judge and gave the Senate with the articles impeachment. And Nixon had been sentenced in a criminal trial. The Senate conjured Impeachment Rule XI, a Senate procedural principle which allows a committee to take evidence and proof with testimony. After the committee finished its procedures and then the Senate voted to convict and expel him from office. The judge afterward challenged against the utilization of a committee to take proof, evidence and testimony abused the Constitution's clause that the Senate "*try*" all impeachments.

The U.S. District Court for the District of Columbia at first tossed out Judge Hastings' Senate impeachment conviction, since the Senate had attempted his impeachment before a committee instead of the full Senate. The judgment was vacated on appeal petition and jailed for reassessment in light of *Nixon v. United States*. Then the district court rejected the suit since it introduced a non-justiciable political

---

[20] The Court listed *"reasons why the Judiciary, and the Supreme Court in particular, were not chosen to have any role in impeachments,"* and elsewhere agreed with the appeals court that *"opening the door of judicial review to the procedures used by the Senate in trying impeachments would expose the political life of the country to months, or perhaps years, of chaos."* 506 U.S. at 234, 236.

question.

So, their hypothetical argument is that the Supreme Court can exercise judicial review in certain circumstances when the Senate applying *"sole power to try impeachment"* and convicts any federal official or the President without a trial.

Pathway of Impeachment Process of Donald Trump

In general, impeachment is portion of the United States' Constitution and it is led by the U.S. House of Representatives and the Senate. Basically, the House of Representatives chooses whether there's sufficient and adequate evidence for a federal official to be tried by the Senate.

Pathway of the House of Representatives

The House of Representatives has widespread scope on how to conduct impeachment. This part discusses various extensive flexible approaches to impeach *Donald Trump* step by step followed by the House of Representatives:

Step 1: House Speaker declares official impeachment inquiry.

Nancy Pelosi, the Speaker of the House of Representatives, proclaims in September the House of Representative will open an official impeachment inquiry against President *Donald*

Trump connected to a whistle-blower complaint claiming troubling connections between Trump and the president of Ukraine forcing the president of Ukraine to investigate presidential candidate Joe Biden and his son Hunter Biden.

Step 2: Six House Committees Investigate.

Now, six committees of the House of Representatives already investigate *Donald Trump*'s impeachment probes under the authority of an official impeachment procedure. The Six committees, i.e., Judiciary Committee, Intelligence Committee, Foreign Affairs Committee, Financial Services Committee, Oversight and Reform Committee and Ways & Means Committee with all Democratic majorities, are investigating the president *Donald Trump* inquiry.

Six Committees are as follows:

Judiciary Committee: This Committee is formed headed by a Democratic Member *Jerry Nadler*. The Judiciary Committee will decide whether to present charges against *Donald Trump* to the full House. Committee on the Judiciary is of 41 Members including 24 from Democrat and 17 from Republican. The Judiciary Committee is investigating and examining Russian interference and intervention in the 2016 U.S. presidential election and finding out links interactions, and relation the Trump election campaign and Russians.

Intelligence Committee: This Committee is also formed headed by a Democratic Member Adam Schiff. The Intelligence Committee is designated as the lead to the impeachment process of the President. Permanent Select Committee on Intelligence is of 22 Members including 13 from Democrat and 9 from Republican. The Intelligence Committee is revising Russian impact on the 2016 U.S. presidential elections and if foreign nations have any leverage, control, influence over *Donald Trump*, his family or his businesses or overall activities.

Foreign Affairs Committee: This Committee is formed headed by a Democratic Member Eliot L. Engel. Committee on Foreign Affairs is of 47 Members including 26 from Democrat and 21 from Republican. Now, the Foreign Affairs Committee is investigating and inspecting *Donald Trump*'s interactions, relation and link with Ukraine.

Financial Services Committee: This Committee is formed headed by a Democratic Member *Maxine Waters*. Committee on Financial Services is of 60 Members including 34 from Democrat and 26 from Republican. Now, the

Financial Services Committee is investigating Trump's connection with Deutsche Bank AG, the German multinational investment bank, and if Russian currency was laundered through *the Deutsche Bank AG.*

Oversight and Reform Committee: This Committee is formed headed by a Democratic Member Carolyn Maloney. Committee on Oversight and Reform is of 39 Members including 22 from Democrat and 17 from Republican. The Oversight and Reform Committee is investigating and inspecting whether Trump violated financial disclosure laws. It summoned Mazars USA, an international accounting firm, for Trump financial records going back to 2009.

Ways & Means Committee: This Committee is formed headed by a Democratic Member Richard Neal. *Ways and Means Committee* is of 47 Members including 25 from Democrat and 17 from Republican. The Ways and Means Committee is looking for six years of Trump's individual and business-related income tax returns.

Each of the six committees including *Judiciary Committee, Intelligence Committee, Foreign Affairs Committee, Financial Services Committee, Oversight and Reform Committee* and *Ways & Means Committee* is concentrating on its extent of expertise and proficiency in a specific portion of the overall and inclusive *Donald Trump* investigation. All of the committees initiated their investigation work on Sept. 24, 2019 when the Speaker of the House of Representatives Nancy Pelosi announced the impeachment inquiry. The first witness *Kurt Volker* is heard on Oct. 2, 2019. *Kurt Volker* is previous special diplomatic envoy to Ukraine. He also met with most of the members of the House intelligence committees, oversight and reform committees, and foreign affairs committees.

Step 3: House votes on how impeachment inquiry will be conducted.

The House of representative passed House Resolution 660 by a tally of 232 to 196 on October 31, 2019 with extent rules for open impeachment hearings held by the Intelligence Committee, though closed testimonies can continue in all six committees. House Resolution 660 guides the all six committees to carry on their inquiries and investigations and permits public release of outcomes or findings and witness testimonies. It also fixes duration on examination and re-examination of witnesses and elaborates in details how witnesses can be summoned.

Figure: 1
House Resolution 660 Partisan Lines

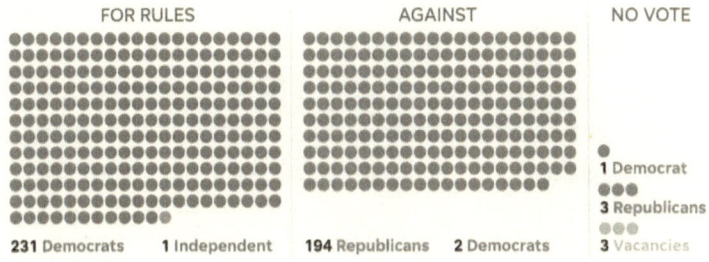

Source:[21]

Step 4: House Intelligence Committee and later the Judiciary Committee, hold public hearing.

The Intelligence Committee of the House of Representatives will arrange public hearings on investigations this month. Then Intelligence Committee of the House of Representatives will inform the collected information by all six committees to the Judiciary Committee. After getting all the investigation reports by all the six committees, will arrange further hearings on what's been found. The accused president and his legal counsel will present their defense against the investigation findings.

---

[21] George Petras, "Pathway of the impeachment process: How it works, where we are", USA TODAY, Nov. 6, 2019, Retrieved from https://www.usatoday.com/ on 07 Nov, 2019

Step 5: Judiciary Committee debates articles of impeachment, voted whether to send to House.

The Judiciary Committee makes the drafts articles of impeachment after debating the all the investigation findings from the six committees investigation. And debate will be held on the president could offer one or more articles of impeachment by the Judiciary Committee. This Judiciary Committee will also debate which, if any, articles of impeachment should be sent to the House. After debating, the Judiciary Committee arrange a vote by simple majority whether to offer the articles to the full House.

Step 6: House votes on whether to impeach. If yes…

After getting the articles of impeachment from the Judiciary Committee, authorization of an impeachment investigation will reach to a vote on the House of Representatives session. And a simple majority will be required to approve at least one article of impeachment to try impeachment trial by the Senate.

Figure 2
Present Scenario of the Position of Democrats and Republicans

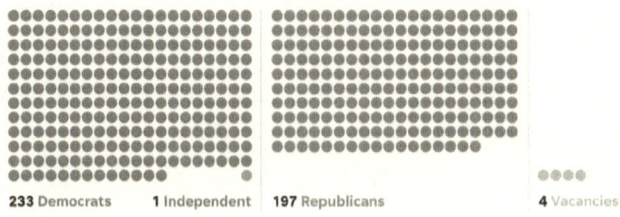

Source: George Petras[22]

At least 218 members votes is essential to impeach the 45th President *Donald Trump* of the full 435-member House. Now there are 4 vacancies; so, 216 votes is needed to impeach the 45th President *Donald Trump* of the current 431 members House. The present scenario shows that any of the articles of impeachment could be passed by the simple majority for the impeachment of the 45th President *Donald Trump* and it shall be to trial in the Senate. If it is not passed any of the articles of impeachment, the impeachment will be ends and President *Donald Trump* will stay in office.

---

[22] George Petras, "Pathway of the impeachment process: How it works, where we are", USA TODAY, Nov. 6, 2019, Retrieved from https://www.usatoday.com/ on 07 Nov, 2019

Pathway of the Senate

If any of the articles of impeachment passes by the majority vote of the House of Representatives and the President is impeached, but not yet removed from *Donald Trump* office. It must go to the Senate, where existing procedures propose that a trial is compulsory by the Senator. The following steps are necessary for the Senate:

Step 1: Senate decides how trial will be conducted.

Senate Majority Leader *Mitch Mcconnell* will conduct the trial process in the Senate.

The Senate agrees a resolution that regulates how the impeachment trial can be conducted, including:

- How much evidence can be presented?
- The number of days the trial can last;
- How many witnesses can be included?

While Democrats control the House of Representatives but Republicans dominates the Senate with 53 Republicans, 47 Democrats and 2 Independent Senator.

Step 2: Trial is held with Senate acting as jury.

Supreme Court's chief justice *John Roberts* presiding this Step. House of Representatives members prosecutes as *'managers'*, assist as prosecutors. Defense lawyers engaged by the accused president defend for him. The full 100 Senators would then become jury in the impeachment trial.

Step 3: Senate renders impeachment verdict.

If two-thirds Senator out of the 100-member Senate that means 67 senators or more senators find the president guilty, the president *Donald Trump* will be removed from office. The vice president then becomes president.

And if less than two-thirds Senator out of the 100-member Senate that means less than 67 senators or less senators find the president guilty, the president *Donald Trump* will not be removed from office. And Senators will not find any guilty, President *Donald Trump* remains in office.

CHAPTER THREE
IMPEACHABLE OFFENSES

What are impeachable offenses?

Impeachment and its possible consequences are stated in Article II, Section 4 of the U.S. Constitution:

> *"The President, Vice President and all civil officers of the United States, shall be removed from office on impeachment for, and conviction of, treason, bribery, or other high crimes and misdemeanors."*

The founders of the U.S. Constitution intentionally kept the four terms used for criminal activity like, *"treason, bribery, or other high crimes and misdemeanors".*

Recent interpreters of the U.S. Constitution have commonly found in this provision the whole extent of the impeachment authority. In any case, a cautious perusing of the language demonstrates that it is neither a meaning of the impeachment authority nor a comprehensive catalogue of impeachable offenses.

In the first scale, all over, the expressions of Article II, § 4, don't imply to be a definition of impeachment. They necessitate the expulsion of federal civil officials convicted or sentenced in impeachment procedures of *"treason, bribery, or other high crimes and misdemeanors." "Shall be removed"* has the type of an order, not of a meaning or definition or description of the impeachment.[23]

In the second scale, the language of Article II, § 4, doesn't show that it is a comprehensive catalogue of impeachable offenses. Those federal civil officials must be evacuated for *"treason, bribery, or other high crimes and misdemeanors,"* doesn't prevent the presence of other offense for which they might be impeached and expelled from their office. For Article II, § 4, to be a complete, comprehensive and exhaustive listing *"shall be removed for"* must be occupied as by identical to *"shall be removed only for."* But when the Framers of the U.S. Constitution desired to provide a limiting definition, they realized how to do so unambiguously, as in their meaning of treason.[24] Thus, equitably read, Article II, § 4, doesn't express definition every impeachable offense, however stipulates determines those offenses for which removal or elimination or evacuation is obligatory.

The term *"treason" and "bribery"* is very clear in the legal concept. But the next two terms *"other high crimes and misdemeanors"* is vague and

---

[23] "Shall" has an imperative and authoritative power wherever in the Constitution when it happens in an independent clause. Each order in the Constitution is framed using the term "Shall." See, e.g., Martin v. Hunter's Lessee, 14 U.S. (1 Wheat.) 304, 328-33 (1816).

[24] U.S. CONsT. art. III, § 3. And *Holmes v. Jennison*, 39 U.S. (14 Pet.) 540, 571 (1840).

ambiguous in the context of legal terminology. The founders of the U.S. Constitution deliberately kept the generic term *"high crimes and misdemeanors"*.

The federal bribery statute U.S. Code § 201 says someone has committed bribery if he or she is a "public official" who

> *"directly or indirectly, corruptly demands, seeks, receives, accepts, or agrees to receive or accept anything of value personally ... in return for ... being influenced in the performance of any official act."*

William Hawkins's 1716[25] "A Treatise of the Pleas of the Crown" expresses the definition of the term "bribery" as

> *"receiving or offering of any undue reward, by or to any person whatsoever, whose ordinary profession or business relates to the administration of public justice, in order to incline him to do a thing against the known rules of honesty and integrity."*

A 1797 list of *"indictable crimes"* in Delaware describes bribery as *"an offense against public justice,"* which contains unnecessary payment for someone in a position of power *"to influence him against the known rules of law, honestly, or integrity"* and adds: *"He who accepts and he who offers the bribe are*

---

[25] William Hawkins's "A Treatise of the Pleas of the Crown," 1716.

both liable to punishment.'[26]

The Framers of the U.S. Constitution dismissed the expression *'maladministration'* as reason or grounds for conviction to impeach. They didn't desire a president hurled out simply in light of the fact that Congress didn't think he was working superbly. Alexander Hamilton said impeachable offenses were those that included maltreatment of public trust. The term is commonly comprehended to mean maltreatment of office that outcome in damage to people in general.

In general, *"high crimes and misdemeanors"* can be whatever the House of Representatives decides ascends to the degree of maltreatment or misuse of office or infringement of public trust. In 1970, at that point congressman and future president, Gerald Ford, stated:

> *"An impeachable offense is whatever a majority of the House of Representatives considers it to be at a given moment in history."*

Raoul Berger presumes that *"high crimes and misdemeanors,"* and thusly impeachable offenses, add up to genuine grave misbehavior, but are not

---

[26] Zephyr Teachout, *Corruption in America*, Harvard University Press, 2014.

constrained to statutory violations.[27]

Recent concept developed for the explanation of those terms *"high crimes and misdemeanors* "comprise just of wrongdoings criminal under federal law and infringement of oaths of office.

Another analyst infers that *"high crimes and misdemeanors"* ought to be reserved to misbehavior, not actually criminal, which creates danger to the organization of government itself.[28]

The standard beginning stage of these observers was so little tested that, nearly as a matter of course, the words *"high crimes and misdemeanors"* have come to be practically identical and synonymous with *"impeachable offenses."*

Almost all of the various other people who composed or talked regarding the matter of indictment or impeachment while differing among themselves over what establishes *"high crimes and misdemeanors"* harmonized that the language of the U.S. Constitution requires *"high crimes and misdemeanors"* as the principle of an impeachment.[29]

---

[27] R. Berger, Impeachment: The Constitutional Problems 53-102 (1973) (esp. 91-93).
[28] C. Black, Impeachment: A Handbook 36-41 (1974)
[29] Fenton, The Scope of the Impeachment Power, 65 Nw. U.L. REV. 719, 720 (1970); Panel on Impeachment, YALE L. REP., Winter 1974, at 25-27.

It is argued in various ways such as,

Firstly, that impeachable offenses are not characterized or defined in the U.S. Constitution,

Secondly, that *"high crimes and misdemeanors"* are a traditionally well-characterized type of offenses pointed explicitly against the state, for which expulsion is obligatory upon conviction by the Senate, that Congress has the ability to impeach and evacuate federal civil officials for a wide scope of genuine offenses other than high crimes and misdemeanors, and

Thirdly, that the Senate can enforce authorizations less extreme than expulsion and removal from office on federal civil officials sentenced for such different offenses.

'High' has denoted crimes against the state since the Middle Ages. 23[30]

For what reason does the Constitution require evacuation for the felonies stated in Article II,

---

[30] This definition of "*high*" first appeared in impeachments in the proceedings against Robert de Vere and Michael de la Pole in 1386: *"[I]t was declared that in so high a crime as is alleged in this appeal, which touches the person of the king, our Lord, and the state of his entire realm .... "* 3 ROTULI PARLIAMENTORUM [Rolls of Parliament] 236 (undated) (emphasis added) (passage from the rolls of Parliament for the years 1387-88, transl. by the author from the original French: *"[estoit declare], Que en sihaute crime come est pretendu en cest Appell, q [qui] touche la persone du Roi fire [nostre] dit Sr [Seigneur], & l'estat de tout son Roialme .... "*

while parting different crimes to the decision of Congress and its long historic impression and observation of the impeachment authority? The appropriate response lies in the importance of the term '*high*'. Without the term '*high*' connected to it, the articulation "*crimes and misdemeanors*" is simply a depiction of general public wrongs, crimes, or felonies which are cognizable in general or common criminal justice system.[31]

A "*high crime or misdemeanor*" isn't only a grave offense, but rather one intended for the sovereign or his administration or government, the most noteworthy forces of the state. The arrangement of the expression of the terms "*treason, bribery, or other high crimes and misdemeanors*" in Article II, § 4 of the U.S. Constitution, shows that "*treason*" and "*bribery*" are "*high*" offenses. The word "*High*" has indicated violations against the nation or state or government since 13th century. At first, this meaning of '*high*' seemed in impeachments procedures against *Robert de Vere* and *Michael de la Pole* in 1386:

> "*[I]t was declared that in so high a crime as is*

---

[31] Blackstone, language of the criminal law, commences: "*We are now arrived at the fourth and last branch of these commentaries, which treats of public wrongs or crimes and misdemeanors.*" He later continues: "*T A crime, or misdemeanor, is an act committed, or omitted, in violation of a public law, either forbidding or commanding it.*" Id. at *5.

alleged in this appeal, which touches the person of the king, our Lord, and the state of his entire realm...."

"*High crimes and misdemeanors*" hence mention to violations which mischief the state in a quick technique and debilitate it's working. For Instances of such crimes are: treason, bribery, obstruction of justice, sabotage, misappropriates the government fund, and embezzling or stealing from the public treasury.

It is, obviously, possible first to recognize the impression that *"high crimes and misdemeanors"* as its horrific nature of the crimes portray impeachable offenses, and afterward continue to give wide substance to those terms, in order that the impeachment authority be a sensible remedy or treatment against criminal. However, the Framers of the U.S. Constitution didn't consider this to be arrangement as a get sack: rather they saw "*high misdemeanors*" as having a constrained, but specialized connotation. This significance definition of *"high misdemeanor"* is most likely the one found in Blackstone. Berger presumes that *"high crimes and misdemeanors"* are expressions of art explicitly depicting impeachable offenses, and bears significance meaning which is exceptional from *"crimes and misdemeanors"* transformed by *"high."*

So, given this denotation of *"high,"* it is

famously sensible and significance meaning for the Constitution, through Article II, § 4.

Without a doubt, it is hard to treat the *"high crimes and misdemeanors"* of Article II, § 4, as a complete meaning of impeachable offenses.

Unless the meaning of the term *"high crimes and misdemeanors"* in common law is not to be abandoned, the presently existing outlook that Article II characterizes the full extent of the impeachment authority would leave in office a President who had committed murder, burglary, assault, extortion or so on other following offenses:

- Murder
- Attempted Murder
- Manslaughter
- Soliciting to commit murder
- Child destruction
- Infanticide
- Causing explosion likely to endanger life or property
- Attempt to cause explosion, making or keeping explosive etc.
- Destroying, damaging or endangering the safety of an aircraft
- Endangering the safety of an aircraft
- Racially-aggravated arson (endangering life)
- Kidnapping
- False imprisonment
- Torture
- Aggravated criminal damage
- Aggravated arson

IMPEACHMENT OF DONALD TRUMP

- Arson
- Hostage-taking
- Hijacking
- Other acts endangering or likely to endanger the safety of an aircraft
- Hijacking of ships
- Endangering safety at aerodromes
- Seizing or exercising control of fixed platforms
- Destroying fixed platforms or endangering their safety
- Other acts endangering or likely to endanger safety navigation
- Offences involving threats
- Offences relating to Channel Tunnel trains and the tunnel system
- Genocide, crimes against humanity, war crimes and related offences other than one involving murder
- Possession of firearm with intent to endanger life
- Possession of firearm with intent to cause fear of violence
- Use of firearm to resist arrest
- Possession of firearm at time of committing or being arrested for offence
- Possession of firearm with criminal intent
- Possession or acquisition of certain prohibited weapons etc.
- Possessing or distributing prohibited weapon or ammunition
- Trespassing with firearm or imitation firearm in a building
- Carrying firearm or imitation firearm in public place
- Shortening a shot gun; conversion of firearm
- Trading in firearms without being registered as firearms dealer
- Selling firearm to person without a certificate
- Repairing, testing etc. firearm without a certificate
- Falsifying certificate etc. with view to acquisition of firearm
- Carrying of any offensive weapon in a public place without lawful authority or reasonable excuse

IMPEACHMENT OF DONALD TRUMP

- Manufacture, sale, hire, offer for sale or hire, exposure or possession for the purpose of sale or hire, or lending or giving to any other person and the importation of flick knives and gravity knives
- Having an article with a blade or a sharp point in a public place without good reason or lawful authority.
- unlawful marketing of knives as suitable for combat, or in ways likely to stimulate or encourage violent behavior
- Aggravated burglary
- Robbery or assault with intent to rob
- Armed robbery
- Assault with weapon with intent to rob
- Blackmail
- Riot
- Violent disorder
- Contamination of goods with intent
- Causing death by dangerous driving
- Causing death by careless driving while under the influence of drink or drugs
- Aggravated vehicle taking resulting in death
- Causing danger to road users
- Attempting to choke, suffocate, strangle etc.
- Destroying or damaging property other than an offence of arson
- Causing miscarriage by poison, instrument
- Making threats to kill
- Wounding or grievous bodily harm with intent to cause grievous bodily harm etc.
- Endangering the safety of railway passengers
- Impeding persons endeavoring to escape wrecks
- Administering chloroform, laudanum etc.
- Administering poison etc. so as to endanger life
- Cruelty to persons under 16

IMPEACHMENT OF DONALD TRUMP

- Aiding and abetting suicide
- Prison mutiny
- Manufacture and supply of scheduled substances
- Fraudulent evasion of controls
- Illegal importation of Class A and B drugs
- Offences in relation to proceeds of drug trafficking
- Offences in relation to money laundering investigations
- Practitioner contravening drug supply regulations
- Cultivation of cannabis plant
- Occupier knowingly permitting drugs offences etc.
- Activities relating to opium
- Drug trafficking offences at sea
- Firing on Revenue vessel
- Making or possession of explosive in suspicious circumstances
- Causing bodily injury by explosives
- Using explosive or corrosives with intent to cause grievous bodily harm
- Hostage taking
- Offences against international protection of nuclear material
- Placing explosives with intent to cause bodily injury
- Membership of proscribed organizations
- Support or meeting of proscribed organizations
- Uniform of proscribed organizations
- Fund-raising for terrorism
- Other offences involving money or property to be used for terrorism
- Disclosure prejudicing, or interference of material relevant to, investigation of terrorism
- Weapons training
- Directing terrorist organization
- Possession of articles for terrorist purposes

IMPEACHMENT OF DONALD TRUMP

- Unlawful collection of information for terrorist purposes
- Incitement of terrorism overseas
- Concealing criminal property
- Involvement in arrangements facilitating the acquisition, retention, use or control of criminal property
- Acquisition, use or possession of criminal property
- Failure to disclose knowledge or suspicion of money laundering: regulated sector
- Failure to disclose knowledge or suspicion of money laundering: nominated officers in the regulated sector
- Failure to disclose knowledge or suspicion of money laundering: other nominated officers
- Tipping off
- Causing or allowing the death of a child or vulnerable adult
- Female circumcision
- Female genital mutilation
- Assisting a girl to mutilate her own genitalia
- Assisting a non-UK person to mutilate overseas a girl's genitalia
- Racially-aggravated assault - ABH or GBH
- Racially-aggravated common assault
- Racially-aggravated criminal damage
- Unlawful wounding
- Assault occasioning actual bodily harm
- Concealment of birth
- Abandonment of children under two
- Criminal damage (other than aggravated criminal damage)
- Possession of firearm without certificate
- Carrying loaded firearm in public place
- Trespassing with a firearm
- Shortening of shotgun or possession of shortened shotgun
- Shortening of smooth bore gun

IMPEACHMENT OF DONALD TRUMP

- Possession or acquisition of shotgun without certificate
- Possession of firearms by person convicted of crime
- Acquisition by or supply of firearms to person denied them
- Dealing in firearms
- Failure to comply with certificate when transferring firearm
- Permitting an escape
- Rescue
- Escaping from lawful custody without force
- Breach of prison
- Harboring escaped prisoners
- Assisting prisoners to escape
- Fraudulent evasion of agricultural levy
- Offender armed or disguised
- Making threats to destroy or damage property
- Possessing anything with intent to destroy or damage property
- Child abduction by connected person
- Child abduction by other person
- Bomb hoax
- Producing or supplying Class C drug
- Possession of a Class C drug with intent to supply
- Fraudulent evasion of controls on Class C drugs
- Illegal importation of Class C drugs
- Possession of Class A drug
- Failure to disclose knowledge or suspicion of money laundering
- Tipping-off in relation to money laundering investigations
- Assaults on officers saving wrecks
- Attempting to injure or alarm the Sovereign
- Assisting illegal entry or harboring persons
- Employment of adults subject to immigration control: penalty notice
- Administering poison with intent to injure etc.

IMPEACHMENT OF DONALD TRUMP

- Neglecting to provide food for or assaulting servants etc.
- Setting spring guns with intent to inflict grievous bodily harm
- Supplying instrument etc. to cause miscarriage
- Endeavoring to conceal a birth
- Failure to disclose information about terrorism
- Circumcision of females
- Breaking or injuring submarine telegraph cables
- Failing to keep dogs under proper control resulting in injury
- Making gunpowder etc. to commit offences
- Stirring up racial hatred
- Sexual offences and offences against children Administering drugs to obtain intercourse
- Procurement of a woman by threats
- Procurement of a woman by false pretenses
- Attempted sexual intercourse with girl under 13
- Procurement of a defective
- Intercourse with a defective
- Incest by man with a girl under 13
- Incest by woman with a girl under 13
- Attempted incest by man with a girl over 13
- Gross indecency between male of 21 or over and male under 16
- Indecent assault on a woman
- Indecent assault on a man
- Abuse of position of trust
- Man living on earnings of prostitution
- Woman exercising control over prostitute
- Living on earnings of male prostitution
- Inciting girl under 16 to have incestuous sexual intercourse
- Ill-treatment of persons of unsound mind
- Abduction of unmarried girl under 18 from parent

IMPEACHMENT OF DONALD TRUMP

- Abduction of unmarried girl under 16 from parent
- Abduction of defective from parent
- Causing prostitution of women
- Procuration of girl under 21
- Detention of woman in brothel
- Permitting girl under 16 to use premises for intercourse
- Permitting defective to use premises for intercourse
- Causing or encouraging prostitution of, intercourse with or indecent assault on girl under 16
- Causing or encouraging prostitution of defective
- Soliciting by men
- Keeping a brothel
- Ill-treatment of patients
- Sexual intercourse with patients
- Sexual assault
- Causing sexual activity without penetration
- Paying for sexual services - penetration of a child aged 16 or 17
- Engaging in sexual activity in the presence of a child
- Causing a child to watch a sexual act
- Child sex offence committed by person under 18
- Meeting child following sexual grooming
- Abuse of trust: sexual activity with a child
- Abuse of position of trust: causing a child to engage in sexual activity
- Abuse of trust: sexual activity in the presence of a child
- Abuse of position of trust: causing a child to watch sexual activity
- Engaging in sexual activity in the presence of a person with a mental disorder
- Causing a person with a mental disorder to watch a sexual act
- Engaging in sexual activity in the presence of a person with a mental disorder

IMPEACHMENT OF DONALD TRUMP

- Causing a person with a mental disorder to watch a sexual act
- Care workers: sexual activity in presence of a person with a mental disorder
- Care workers: causing a person with a mental disorder to watch a sexual act
- Causing or inciting prostitution for gain
- Controlling prostitution for gain
- Administering a substance with intent
- Committing offence with intent to commit sexual offence
- Trespass with intent to commit sexual offence
- Sex with adult relative: penetration
- Sex with adult relative: consenting to penetration
- Exposure
- Voyeurism
- Intercourse with an animal
- Sexual penetration of a corpse
- Cruelty to children
- Burglary
- Burglary (domestic)
- Aggravated burglary
- Going equipped to steal
- Burglary with intent to inflict GBH on a person or do unlawful damage to a building or anything in it (dwelling)
- Burglary with intent to inflict GBH on a person or do unlawful damage to a building or anything in it (non-dwelling)
- Burglary with intent to commit rape (dwelling)
- Burglary with intent to commit rape (non-dwelling)
- Burglary (non-domestic)
- Destruction of registers of births etc.
- Making false entries in copies of registers sent to register
- Possession (with intention) of false identity documents

- Possession (with intention) of apparatus or material for making false identity documents
- Possession (without reasonable excuse) of false identity documents or apparatus or material for making false identity documents
- Counterfeiting notes and coins
- Passing counterfeit notes and coins
- Offences involving custody or control of counterfeit notes and coins
- Making, custody or control of counterfeiting materials etc.
- Illegal importation: counterfeit notes or coins
- Fraudulent evasion: counterfeit notes or coins
- VAT offences
- Fraudulent evasion of duty
- Theft
- Removal of articles from places open to the public
- Abstraction of electricity
- Obtaining property by deception
- Obtaining pecuniary advantage by deception
- False accounting
- Handling stolen goods
- Obtaining services by deception
- Evasion of liability by deception
- Illegal importation: not elsewhere specified
- Counterfeiting Customs documents
- Fraudulent evasion: not elsewhere specified
- Forgery
- Copying false instrument with intent
- Using a false instrument
- Using a copy of a false instrument
- Custody or control of false instruments etc.
- Offences in relation to dies or stamps

IMPEACHMENT OF DONALD TRUMP

- Counterfeiting of dies or marks
- Fraud by false representation
- Fraud by failing to disclose information
- Fraud by abuse of position
- Possession etc. of articles for use in frauds
- Making or supplying articles for use in frauds
- Participating in fraudulent business carried on by sole trader etc.
- Obtaining services dishonestly
- Breach of anti-social behavior order
- Breach of community sentences - Increase the severity of the existing sentence or Revoke the existing sentence and proceed as though sentencing for the original offence.
- Breach of sex offender order
- Racially-aggravated public order offence
- Racially aggravated harassment/putting another in fear of violence
- Having an article with a blade or point in a public place
- Breach of harassment injunction
- Putting people in fear of violence
- Offences in relation to certain dangerous articles
- Breach of restraining order
- Being drunk on an aircraft
- Possession of offensive weapon
- Affray
- Assault with intent to resist arrest
- Unlawful eviction and harassment of occupier
- Fraudulent evasion of the prohibition on importing indecent or obscene articles
- Obscene articles intended for publication for gain
- Gross indecency between males (other than where one is 21 or over and the other is under 16)
- Solicitation for immoral purposes

IMPEACHMENT OF DONALD TRUMP

- Buggery of males of 16 or over otherwise than in private
- Acts outraging public decency
- Offences of publication of obscene matter
- Keeping a disorderly house
- Indecent display
- Presentation of obscene performance
- Procurement of intercourse by threats etc.
- Causing prostitution of women
- Detention of woman in brothel or other premises
- Procurement of a woman by false pretenses
- Procuring others to commit homosexual acts
- Trade description offences
- Misconduct endangering ship or persons on board ship
- Obstructing engine or carriage on railway
- Offences relating to the safe custody of controlled drugs
- Possession of Class B or C drug
- Wanton or furious driving
- Dangerous driving
- Forgery and misuse of driving documents
- Forgery of driving documents
- Forgery etc. of licenses and other documents
- Mishandling or falsifying parking documents etc.
- Aggravated vehicle taking
- Failing to stop or failing to report
- Failing to nominate a driver at the time of an alleged offence
- Forgery, alteration, fraud of licenses etc.
- Making off without payment
- Agreeing to indemnify sureties
- Sending prohibited articles by post
- Impersonating Customs officer

IMPEACHMENT OF DONALD TRUMP

- Obstructing Customs officer
- Offences against public justice and similar offences
- Conspiring to commit offences outside the United Kingdom
- Perverting the course of public justice
- Perjuries
- Corrupt transactions with agents
- Corruption in public office
- Embracery
- Fabrication of evidence with intent to mislead a tribunal
- Personation of jurors
- Concealing an arrestable offence
- Assisting offenders
- False evidence before European Court
- Personating for purposes of bail etc.
- Intimidating a witness, juror etc.
- Harming, threatening to harm a witness, juror etc.
- Prejudicing a drug trafficking investigation
- Giving false statements to procure cremation
- False statement
- Making a false statement to obtain interim possession order
- Making false statement to resist making of interim possession order
- Making false statement to authorized officer
- Rape
- Sexual intercourse with girl under 13
- Attempted sexual intercourse with girl under 13
- Sexual intercourse with defective
- Incest by man with a girl under 13
- Buggery of person under 16
- Indecency with children under 14
- Taking, having etc. indecent photographs of children

IMPEACHMENT OF DONALD TRUMP

- Possession of indecent photograph of a child
- Assault with intent to commit buggery
- Abduction of woman by force
- Permitting girl under 13 to use premises for sexual intercourse
- Allowing or procuring child under 16 to go abroad to perform
- Abduction of unmarried girl under 16 from parent
- Permitting girl under 16 to use premises for intercourse
- Causing or encouraging prostitution of girl under 16
- Rape
- Assault by penetration
- Sexual assault
- Causing a person to engage in sexual activity without consent
- Rape of child under 13
- Assault of child under 13 by penetration
- Sexual assault of child under 13
- Causing a child under 13 to engage in sexual activity
- Sexual activity with a child
- Causing a child to engage in sexual activity
- Arranging or facilitating commission of a child sex offence
- Sexual activity with a child family member, with penetration (Offender over 18)
- Sexual activity with a child family member, with penetration (Offender under 18)
- Inciting a child family member to engage in sexual activity (Offender over 18)
- Inciting a child family member to engage in sexual activity (Offender under 18)
- Sexual activity with a person with a mental disorder
- Causing or inciting a person with a mental disorder to engage in sexual activity

- Engaging in sexual activity in the presence of a person with a mental disorder impeding choice
- Causing a person with a mental disorder impeding choice to watch a sexual act
- Inducement, threat or deception to procure sexual activity with a person with a mental disorder
- Inducing person with mental disorder to engage in sexual activity
- Engaging in sexual activity in the presence, procured by inducement, threat or deception, of a person with a mental disorder
- Causing a person with a mental disorder to watch a sexual act by inducement, threat or deception
- Care workers: sexual activity with a person with a mental disorder
- Care workers: inciting person with mental disorder to engage in sexual act
- Paying for sexual services - penetration - of a child under 13
- Paying for sexual services - penetration - of a child under 16
- Causing or inciting child prostitution or pornography
- Controlling a child prostitute
- Facilitating child prostitution
- Trafficking into UK for sexual exploitation
- Trafficking within UK for sexual exploitation
- Trafficking out of UK for sexual exploitation

There is a confusion to include above all the enlisted crime to be impeachable offences under the expression *"high crimes and misdemeanors"*. Brant provides murder and rape as *"manifest grounds of removal for high crimes."*[82] But murder and rape are directed at individuals, and were not *"high"* at

---

[32] Raoul Berger, *Impeachment: The Constitutional Problems,* Harvard University Press, 1973, p. 43.

common law.

Undoubtedly, Article II, § 1, of the U.S. Constitution gives that on account of the President's *"incapability"* his office will lapse upon the Vice President. In any case, nothing there shows that there is any method of evacuation other than impeachment. The very circumstance that the Constitution seems to face expulsion for *"inability"* fortifies the *"imperative"* hypothesis of Article II, § 4, exhibited in this Memo.

Smith, First Congress Rep. Smith of South Carolina, was confidently mentioning to Article II, § 1, and his structure of this provision is inconceivable except if he recognized that the extent of impeachment went beyond the expressions of Article II, § 4.

In comprehensively, a close perusing of the U.S. Constitution uncovers that the extent of latitude and longitude of the impeachment authority isn't described in definition in that charter. If Article I allows the ability to impeach as that power was comprehended in 1787, at that point the scope of impeachable felonies is brightened, not by those offenses for which expulsion of any federal officials is made compulsory in Article II, but by the comprehension of the impeachment power in United Kingdom and United States of America during the time of the drafting of the Constitution in 1787.

CHAPTER FOUR
PREVIOUS IMPEACHMENT FACTS

Previous impeachment investigations and results

The House of Representatives has commenced impeachment proceedings 62 times since the adoption of the Constitution in 1789. The House has impeached 19 federal civil officers including 15 federal judges (including thirteen district court judges, one court of appeals judge (who also sat on the Commerce Court), and one Supreme Court Associate Justice Samuel Chase in 1804), one Senator William Blount of Tennessee on July 7, 1797,[33] one Cabinet member Secretary of War William W. Belknap in 1876, and two Presidents - Andrew Johnson and Bill Clinton; both were later acquitted by the Senate.[34] The Senate has conducted 16[35] full impeachment trials.[36] Of

---

[33] The Senate did not hold a trial but, the day after Blount's impeachment, voted 25–1 to expel him for *"being guilty of a high misdemeanor, entirely inconsistent with his public trust and duty as a Senator."*

[34] House Practice, at 609.

[35] Three individuals were impeached, but resigned before completion of the resulting Senate trial.

[36] *See Report of the Impeachment Trial Committee On the Articles Against Judge G. Thomas Porteous, Jr.* 1 n.1, S.Rept. 111-347 (2010). Impeachment trials were conducted for William Blount, United States Senator from Tennessee (impeachment proceedings from 1797-1799); John Pickering, District Judge for the United States District Court for the District of New Hampshire (1803-1804); Samuel Chase, Associate Justice of the United States Supreme Court (1804-1805); James H. Peck, District Judge for the United States District Court for the District of Missouri (1826-1831); West H. Humphreys, District Judge for the United States District Court for

these, eight individuals—all federal judges—were convicted by the Senate.[37] 15 of these article of impeachment cases resulted in impeachment by the House of Representative—President Andrew Johnson in 1868, Secretary of War William W. Belknap in 1876, Senator William Blount in 1799 and 12 federal judges. Only seven impeachments have led to Senate convictions—all of federal judges. For instances, in which an impeachment procedure initiated but did not result in impeachment.

The following 19 federal officials has been

---

the District of Tennessee (1862); Andrew Johnson, President of the United States (1867-1868); William W. Belknap, Secretary of War (1876); Charles Swayne, District Judge for the United States District Court for the Northern District of Florida (1903-1905); Robert W. Archbald, Circuit Judge for the United States Court of Appeals for the Third Circuit, serving as Associate Judge for the United States Commerce Court (1912-1913); Harold Louderback, District Judge for the United States District Court for the Northern District of California (1932-1933); Halsted Ritter, District Judge for the United States District Court for the Southern District of Florida (1936); Harry E. Claiborne, District Judge for the United States District Court for the District of Nevada (1986); Alcee Hastings, United States District Judge for the Southern District of Florida (1988-1989); Walter L. Nixon, Jr., United States District Judge for the Southern District of Mississippi (1988-1989); William Jefferson Clinton, President of the United States (1998); and G. Thomas Porteous, United States District Judge for the Eastern District of Louisiana (2010).

[37] John Pickering (1804); West H. Humphreys (1862); Robert W. Archbald (1913); Halsted Ritter (1936); Harry E. Claiborne (1986); Alcee Hastings (1989); Walter L. Nixon, Jr. (1989); G. Thomas Porteous (2010). *See Porteous Impeachment, supra note* 5, at 1 n.1.

initiated impeachment proceedings and conferred to a committee of the House of Representatives.

Firstly, on July 7, 1797 William Blount was impeached for conspiring to assist Britain in capturing Spanish territory. William Blount was a Senator of Tennessee, United States. Senate refused to accept impeachment of a Senator by the House of Representatives, instead expelling him from the Senate on their own authority.[38]

Secondly, on March 2, 1803, John Pickering was impeached for Drunkenness and unlawful rulings. John Pickering was a Judge (District of New Hampshire). John Pickering was convicted and removed on March 12, 1804. He was the first federal official to be discharged from office upon conviction of drunkenness and unlawful rulings by impeachment. John Pickering engaged as chief justice of the New Hampshire Superior Court of Judicature and as judge for the United States District

---

[38] Chapter 4: Complete List of Senate Impeachment Trials". United States Senate. Archived from the original on December 2, 2010. Retrieved December 8, 2018.

Court for the District of New Hampshire.

Thirdly, on March 12, 1804, Samuel Chase was impeached by the House of Representative on grounds of political bias and arbitrary rulings, promoting a partisan political agenda on the bench but was acquitted by the Senate on March 1, 1805 for not proving the ground of article of impeachment on letting his partisan leanings affect his court decisions and continued in office. He was Associate Justice of Supreme Court of the United States.

Fourthly, on April 24, 1830, James H. Peck Judge (District of Missouri) was impeached by the House of Representatives, on a charge of abuse of the contempt power and abuse of power. The Senate of United States initiated his impeachment trial on April 26, 1830, and acquitted him on January 31, 1831, with 21 voting guilty and 22 voting not guilty. He was a United States District Judge of the United States District Court for the District of Missouri.

Fifthly, on May 6, 1862, West Hughes Humphreys was impeached by the House of Representatives, on a charge of openly calling for secession; providing assistance to an equipped with arms rebellion; collaborating with Jefferson Davis; serving as a Confederate judge; confiscating the property of Military Governor Andrew Johnson and United States Supreme Court Justice John Catron; and imprisoning a Union supporter with *"intent to injure him."* He was Judge of Eastern, Middle, and Western Districts of Tennessee. And on June 26, 1862, the United States Senate initiated the trial of the impeachment in his absence and later that day unanimously condemned him of all charges presented, except that of confiscating the property of Andrew Johnson. His judgeship terminated on June 26, 1862, due to impeachment, conviction. And lastly removed from his office.

Sixthly, on February 24, 1868, Andrew Johnson was impeached by the House of Representatives, on a charge of Violating the Tenure of Office Act. He was 17th President of the United States. The United States Senate acquitted on May 26, 1868, 35–19 in favor of conviction, falling one vote short of two-thirds for not proving the ground of article of impeachment.

Seventhly, on February 28, 1873, Mark W. Delahay was impeached by the House of Representatives, on a charge of drunkenness. Mark William Delahay was a United States District Judge of the United States District Court for the District of Kansas. District Judge of Kansas Mark W. Delahay resigned on December 12, 1873 after being impeached by the United States House of Representatives due to allegations of alcoholism.

Eighthly, on March 2, 1876, William W. Belknap was impeached by the House of Representatives, on a charge of graft, corruption by getting profits from traderships reached Representative

Hiester Clymer, chairman of the Committee on Expenditures in the Department of War. He was United States Secretary of War. But he resigned after impeachment by the United States House of Representatives due to graft, corruption and before initiated trial in the Senate. He was acquitted by the Senate after his resignation on August 1, 1876.

Ninthly, on December 13, 1904, Charles Swayne was impeached by the House of Representatives, on a charge of filing feck travel receipts, improper utilize of private railroad cars, illegally imprisoning two attorneys for contempt, and living outside of his district. He was Judge of Northern District of Florida. He was acquitted by the Senate after his resignation on February 27, 1905 found not guilty for failure to live in his district and abuse of power.

Tenthly, on July 11, 1912, Robert Wodrow Archbald was impeached by the House of Representatives, on a charge of improper acceptance of gifts from litigants and attorneys. The Senate convicted him of five of the 13 articles of impeachment on January 13, 1913. The

Senate then removed and disqualified on January 13, 1913 him from further office by a vote of 68 to 5. He was an Associate Justice (United States Commerce Court) Judge (Third Circuit Court of Appeals).

Eleventh, on April 1, 1926, George W. English was impeached by the House of Representatives, on a charge of abuse of power. George Washington English was a United States District Judge of the United States District Court for the Eastern District of Illinois. He Resigned on November 4, 1926 and the Senate then removed and disqualified by the proceedings on December 13, 1926.

Twelfth, on February 24, 1933, Harold Louderback, eleventh federal official to be served with articles of Impeachment, was impeached by the House of Representatives, on a charge of corruption. He was Judge, Northern District of California. But he was acquitted in the Senate on May 24, 1933 and returned to the bench.

Thirteenth, on March 2, 1936 Halsted Ritter was impeached by the House of Representatives, on a charge of champerty, corruption, tax evasion, practicing law while a judge. He was a Judge at Southern District of Florida. He was convicted and removed on April 17, 1936 by the Senate. He was the thirteenth federal official to be impeached by the House of Representatives and the fourth federal official to be convicted and removed from office by the United States Senate. He was a United States District Judge of the United States District Court for the Southern District of Florida.

Fourteenth, on July 22, 1986, Harry E. Claiborne was impeached by the House of Representatives, on a charge of Tax evasion. He was only the fifth federal official in United States history to be removed from office through impeachment by the House of Representatives and the Senate was dismissed and removed on October 9, 1986. He was the first federal judge to be sent to prison.

Fifteenth, on August 3, 1988, Alcee Hastings was impeached by the House of Representatives, on a charge of accepting a bribe, and committing perjury during the resulting investigation. The Senate was dismissed and removed on October 20, 1989. He was Judge, Southern District of Florida.

Sixteenth, on May 10, 1989, Walter Nixon was impeached by the House of Representatives, on a charge of perjury. The Senate was convicted for committing perjury before a grand jury. Upon his conviction by the Senate, he was removed from office on November 3, 1989. He was the Chief Judge of the United States District Court for the Southern District of Mississippi.

Seventeenth, on December 19, 1998, William Jefferson Clinton known as Bill Clinton was impeached by the House of Representatives, on a charge of perjury to a grand jury voted 228-206 and voted 221-212 to impeach him for obstruction of justice. After the Andrew Johnson impeachment, Bill Clinton was only the second U.S. president to be impeached.

Impeachment proceedings were grounded on accusations that Bill Clinton had illegitimately lied about and concealing his affair with 22-year-old White House employee Monica Lewinsky. And then, he was acquitted by the Senate on February 12, 1999 in case of Perjury voted 50–50 and in case of obstruction of justice voted 45–55.

Eighteenth, on June 19, 2009, Samuel B. Kent was impeached by the House of Representatives, on a charge of Sexual assault, and obstruction of justice during the resulting investigation. He was Judge of the United States District Court for the Southern District of Texas. He resigned on June 30, 2009, proceedings dismissed on July 22, 2009.

Nineteenth, on March 11, 2010, Thomas Porteous was impeached by the House of Representatives, on a charge of Making false financial disclosures, corruption. He was convicted, removed and disqualified by the senate on December 8, 2010. He was Judge of the United States District Court for the Eastern District of Louisiana.

Lastly, but it is not Twentieth, it is ongoing impeachment process of *"Donald Trump"*. On September 24, 2019, the House of Representatives has taken initiative of impeachment 45th President of the United States *Donald J. Trump* by enlisting the assistance of foreign governments with re-election. Financial Services, the Judiciary, Intelligence, Foreign Affairs, Oversight and Reform, and Ways and Means committees undertaking an impeachment inquiry beginning on September 24, 2019. The inquiry is currently continuing.

There have been failed tries to begin impeachment proceedings against John Tyler, Richard Nixon, George W. Bush and Barack Obama.

Steady with the English knowledge and practice and the comprehension of America's Founders, at least 11 of these 19 impeachments included articles charging noncriminal offense.[39] Put in an unexpected way, 33% of the articles introduced in those impeachments *"explicitly charged the violation of a criminal statute."*[40] Of the 19

---

[39] House Practice, at 612.
[40] *Id.*; U.S. Constitution Annotated, at 650 *("Debate prior to adoption of the phrase and comments thereafter in the ratifying conventions were to the effect*

impeachments by the House of Representatives, two cases didn't originate to trial because the civil officials had left office, seven were acquitted by the Senate, and eight federal civil officers were sentenced by different term, every one of whom were judges.

Moreover, an impeachment procedure against Richard Nixon was started; however, it is not finished, as he left office before the full House decided on the articles of impeachment. After all, to date, no president has been expelled from office by impeachment and conviction.

But the 45th American most powerful President *Donald J. Trump* could be the third?

---

that the President (all the debate was in terms of the President) should be removable by impeachment for commissions or omissions in office which were not criminally cognizable.").

CHAPTER FIVE

GROUNDS FOR IMPEACHMENT OF DONALD TRUMP

General Grounds for Impeachment of Donald Trump

The Constitution of the United States of America does not define impeachment but it only typify the grounds and justification for impeachment and conviction as *"Treason, Bribery, or other high Crimes and Misdemeanors."* At the point, when the House of Representatives verifies that reason for impeachment be present, and they are involved by the House of Representative, they are exhibited to the Senate by making articles of impeachment. Any of the articles may give an adequate foundation or ground for impeachment.

The literal explanation which has been set on the terms *"high Crimes and Misdemeanors"* is a wide-ranging and spacious meaning. The originators of the U.S. Constitution received the expression from the English practice. During the Constitutional Convention, the expression of the terms *"high crimes and misdemeanors"* had been utilize for more than 400 years in impeachment procedures in Parliament. A few of these impeachments occurred by high impeachments; others occurred for the conviction of high crimes and misdemeanors.

Lastly, it is comprised both statutory crimes and non-statutory offenses as the impeachment grounds. A significant number of the charges included maltreatment of official authority, belief or trust.

A crime must be severe or considerable in nature to give grounds for impeachment. This prerequisite comes from the speech of the statement itself——*"'high Crimes and Misdemeanors.'"*. While there is some power to the contradictory, it is commonly acknowledged that the modifier *"high"* modifies "Misdemeanors" and also *"Crimes."* [41]

Regarding what comprises a genuine, impeachable offense, one analyst has stated: [42]

> *"To determine whether or not an act or a course of conduct is sufficient in law to support an impeachment, resort must be had to the eternal principles of right, applied to public propriety and civil morality. The offense must be prejudicial to the public interest and it must flow from a willful intent, or a reckless disregard of duty. . . . It may constitute an intentional violation of positive law, or it may be an official dereliction of commission or omission, a serious breach of moral obligation, or other gross impropriety of personal conduct which, in its natural consequences, tends to bring an office into contempt and disrepute."*

---

[41] Impeachment—Selected Materials, Committee on the Judiciary, 93–1, Oct. 1973, p 682.
[42] Brown, The Impeachment of the Federal Judiciary, 26 Harv. L. Rev. 684, 703, 704.

Donald Trump's Impeachable Offenses

No impeachment procedure could practically incorporate all the crimes or offences or misdeeds or misbehave thing of the 45th American President *Donald Trump* has committed. The House of Representatives Democrats should settle down no more 10 (ten) crimes that may, together, recount to an anecdote about how much *Donald Trump*'s Republican followers are eager to endure in the almost three years' duration of the Trump's administration of their disparity driving list of items —from the president's private graft and endeavors to destabilize the standard of law and violation of rule of law and American traditional presidential elections to the discrimination of his heartless nature and maybe even criminal immigration plan.

All things considered, these are very poor explanations to have the Ukraine substances, which is really upsetting, supersede crimes that could make up a more extensive way for impeachment of the 45th President *Donald Trump*. While more articles of impeachment against *Donald Trump* aren't bound to prompt his removal or discharge than a narrower way, an inclusive impeachment would all the more entirely satisfy

Congress' constitutional commitment- *"[t]he President, Vice President and all civil officers of the United States, shall be removed from office on impeachment for, and conviction of, treason, bribery, or other high crimes and misdemeanors"*[43] to grip the American president responsible. Not exclusively would a case so inferred be more diligently to dismiss or disregard, the appearance of such a claim *"Ukraine Phone Calling"* against Trump may inconvenience various voters in various manners—and defenseless Republicans would be compelled to react to numerous offenses.

The Democratic Party of the USA should hold hearings and draft articles of impeachment on the Ukraine scandal. They must to also consider responsibility similar on the following more 10 unexpected occurrences by the 45th President:

1. Donald Trump's obstruction of Justice

Robert Mueller's team did scrutinize 10 (ten) distinct activities in which *Donald Trump* may have done obstruction of Justice during the investigation of Russian interference in the 2016 campaign.

U.S. Code § 1505 is defined *"Obstruction of proceedings before departments, agencies, and committees"*

---

[43] Article II, Section 4 of the U.S. Constitution.

as following:

> *"Whoever, with intent to avoid, evade, prevent, or obstruct compliance, in whole or in part, with any civil investigative demand duly and properly made under the Antitrust Civil Process Act, willfully withholds, misrepresents, removes from any place, conceals, covers up, destroys, mutilates, alters, or by other means falsifies any documentary material, answers to written interrogatories, or oral testimony, which is the subject of such demand; or attempts to do so or solicits another to do so; or*
>
> *Whoever corruptly, or by threats or force, or by any threatening letter or communication influences, obstructs, or impedes or endeavors to influence, obstruct, or impede the due and proper administration of the law under which any pending proceeding is being had before any department or agency of the United States, or the due and proper exercise of the power of inquiry under which any inquiry or investigation is being had by either House, or any committee of either House or any joint committee of the Congress—*
>
> *Shall be fined under this title, imprisoned not more than 5 years or, if the offense involves international or domestic terrorism (as defined in section 2331), imprisoned not more than 8 years, or both."*

Frankly said that which activation may be considered as *"obstruction of justice"* is very complex matter. As a law professor I can provide a lot of evidences of *"obstruction of justice"* which was committed by the President Donald Trump. Such as, bribing a judge, destroying evidence, to influence investigations, fired Comey for *"corrupt"* etc. are definitive instances of the crime of *"obstruction of justice"* under the Federal Code.

Then a lot of evidence has submitted by Robert Mueller's investigation which discovered more than 10 occurrences where there was *"very substantial"* evidence that Trump had committed obstruction of justice.

According to the Mueller report, there are the 10 times committed obstruction of justice, such as,

> *"Conduct involving FBI Director Comey and Michael Flynn"; "The President's reaction to the continuing Russia investigation"; "The President's termination of Comey"; "The appointment of Special Counsel and efforts to remove him"; "Efforts to curtail the Special Counsel's investigation"; "Efforts to prevent public disclosure of evidence"; "Further efforts to have the Attorney General take control of the investigation"; "Efforts to have McGahn deny that the President had ordered him to have the Special Counsel removed"; "Conduct towards Flynn, Manafort, [Redacted]" and*

"Conduct involving Michael Cohen". [44]

However, the impeachment investigation did produce definite examples of obstruction of justice that Democrats should noticeably include in their articles of impeachment **"Obstruction of Justice".**

2. Profiting from the Presidency and Violating Emoluments Clause

Article I, Section 9, Clause 8 of the United States Constitution is provided by an arrangement for Nobility Clause using the title *"No Title of Nobility shall be granted by the United States"* that forbids the federal government from giving titles of honorability, and limits any government officials from getting gifts or financial benefits, emoluments or payments, workplaces or titles from outside states and governments without the assent of the United States Congress. This provision is called the *"Emoluments Clause",* it was intended to safeguard the federal government officeholders of the United States against purported *"corrupting foreign influences."*

This Constitution's Foreign Emoluments

---

[44] Will Rahn, "10 Times Trump May Have Obstructed Justice, According To Mueller", CBSNEWS, July 23, 2019, Retrieved From Https://Www.cbsnews.Com/

Clause forbids the American President from taking personal gaining or benefits from any foreign government or official. Article I, Section 9, Clause 8 of the United States Constitution states that-

> *"And no Person holding any Office of Profit or Trust under them, shall, without the Consent of the Congress, accept of any present, Emolument, Office, or Title, of any kind whatever, from any King, Prince, or foreign State."*

In the *New York Times, Zephyr Teachout* in his article *"Trump's Foreign Business Ties May Violate the Constitution"* has opined that the broad business and land dealings of President Donald Trump, particularly as for government organizations in different nations, may fall inside the provision's scope of Emoluments Clause under Article I, Section 9, Clause 8 of the United States Constitution[45].

Three years into *Donald Trump* presidency and administration, he keeps on profiting from belongings and permitting business deals in more than 30 nations around the globe, blowing the blazes of anxieties that the *Donald Trump* government is answerable to remarkable degrees

---

[45] Teachout, Zephyr. "Trump's Foreign Business Ties May Violate the Constitution". *New York Times,* (November 17, 2016.

of foreign influence by financial gaining. *Donald Trump*'s business involvements keep on leaving him with positions, resources, trademarks and different business interests in more than of 30 nations. Such as, *Israel, United Arab Emirates, Scotland, Ireland, Azerbaijan, Turkey, Mexico, Canada, Uruguay, Argentina, Saudi Arabia, Bermuda, St. Martin, Brazil, St. Vincent, Dominican Republic, South Korea, Indonesia, Russia, Philippines, India, Georgia, China, Panama,* and *Qatar.*

Figure 3

Foreign Influence and the Trump Administration

Source: Karl Evers-Hillstrom[46]

---

[46] Karl Evers-Hillstrom, "Foreign Influence and the Trump

As of October 2019, three separate claims were pending in different government courts:

1) *CREW v. Trump, D.C.* : it is a case that is filed Citizens for Responsibility and Ethics (CREW)before the United States District Court for the Southern District of New York on January 23, 2017 by complaining for Defendant President *Donald Trump* has committed and will commit violations of both the Foreign Emoluments Clause and the Domestic Emoluments Clause. These defilements of both the Foreign Emoluments Clause and the Domestic Emoluments Clause includes the followings:

(a) Leasing New York's Trump Tower to the foreign-government-possessed bodies;

(b) President Donald Trump's gained financial benefits by using his own Washington, D.C. inn and eatery for room reservations, eatery purchases, the utilization of conveniences, and the buying of different services and products by foreign governments and ambassadors, state governments, and bureaucratic agencies;

(c) Property interests or different business interactions attached to foreign governments in various different nations;

Administration", Flourish team, 5 Jun 2019.

(d) *Payments from foreign government-possessed TV presenters identified with rebroadcasts and foreign types of the TV program "The Apprentice" and its side projects;*

2) *D.C. and Maryland v. Trump*: The D.C. and Maryland lawsuit is the first time a government entity has sued on June 12, 2017 in the United States District Court for the District of Maryland an American President *Donald Trump* for violating the Emoluments Clause.

3) *Richard Blumenthal, et al. v. Donald J. Trump*: In this case, Richard Blumenthal with 30 Senators and 166 House of Representatives' members filed an allegation for violating Foreign Emoluments Clause of the United States Constitution.

Here, I shortly presented the more violations of Constitutional Emoluments Clause by the 45th American President *Donald Trump*:

In *Israel*, *Trump* Vodka's sales in Israel $50,000 and $100,000 in royalties hasn't described revenue since 2015. And *Elite Tower*, earlier it was familiar as *Trump Plaza Tower* and *Trump Elite Tower*, in *Tel Aviv, Israel*, sold the property for roughly $80 million in 2007 by *Donald Trump*.

In *United Arab Emirates*, *Donald Trump International Golf Club* in *Dubai* inaugurated in February 2017. *Eric Trump* and *Donald Trump Jr.*

toured to Dubai to celebrate the course's inaugural program of the Trump International Golf Club bearing the Secret Service $250,000 cost. *Donald Trump* just presented the respected Presidential Medal of Freedom to the *Donald Trump* Dubai golf course's instructor Tiger Woods.

In *Scotland*, maybe no other foreign nation gives more cash to Trump than Scotland, where the president *Donald Trump* claims two golf courses that got up to $27 million in income a year ago.

In *Ireland*, President *Donald Trump*'s June 2019 tour to Ireland seemed to be in suspicion when *Trump*'s stayed a few days at *Trump International Golf Links Doonbeg*, which income generated $12.5 million to $14.5 within a year.

In *Azerbaijan*, the 33-story tower which is known *"Trump International Hotel & Tower Baku"* is a source of money laundering issue.

In *Turkey*, a little conflict of interest occurred regarding Trump Towers Istanbul. The Trump Towers Istanbul has been licensing under the regime of Turkish President *Tayyip Erdoğan* in 2012 which revenue touched between $100,001 and $1,000,000 last year.

In *Mexico*, *Trump* supposedly collected $32.5 million building a wall between the U.S. and Mexico.

In *Canada*, *Donald Trump Jr.* and Eric Trump commended the inaugural of the 63-storoid tower named *"Trump International Hotel and Tower"* in Vancouver on February 2017. Within one year of presidency of *Donald Trump*, the 63-storoid tower has raking $5 million from $213,946.

In *Uruguay*, *Trump*'s business interests in Uruguay by making building around Uruguayan beach town *Punta del Este*, which had reached the 25th floor of the 26-story tower on January 2017.

In *Argentina*, Trump has kept a hot and cold business relationship for decades of history with Argentine President *Mauricio Macri*. *Donald Trump* was *"true intellectual author"* of the crime in the kidnapping case of Argentine.[47]

In *Saudi Arabia*, there were reports of *Saudi Arabia* in a roundabout way piping assets to *Donald Trump* through Trump organizations, for example, his hotels and restaurants, which might be in the cross of the Emoluments Clause.

---

[47] Anna Massoglia and Karl Evers-Hillstrom, "World of Influence: A guide to Trump's foreign business interests", OpenSecrets.org, June 4, 2019

In *Bermuda*, *D.J. Aerospace Ltd* remains masked in secret. Owning a Boeing 727 luxury airplane with Bermuda registration 'VP-B' entangled a relationship with Bermuda, which is the gross violation of the Emoluments Clause.

In *St. Martin*, there is Trump's comfortable beachside land. After taking oath as the President, this property's value reached $16.9 million to up to $50 million.

In *Brazil*, the Trump Organization's inclusion in an extravagance *Rio de Janeiro* inn apparently reached a sudden conclusion after it was uncovered the undertaking may have had questionable beginnings. Lastly, Trump Towers Rio's partner *Paulo Figueiredo Filho* was charged suspicious investments in the hotel and numerous other real estate schemes from state-owned pension funds and a Brazilian *Arthur César de Menezes Soares Filho* was also charged in a suspected bribery scheme related to the 2016 Olympic Games. Those two Brazilian accused are presently live in the USA with using the topmost guard of President *Donald Trump*.

In *St. Vincent*, President *Donald Trump*'s properties including a resort casino and golf course in *Canouan* were not registered on his most recent financial release.

In *Dominican Republic*, *Eric Trump* toured to journey the project of *Trump Farallon* Estates at Cap Cana after weeks of Trump's presidential inauguration.

In *South Korea*, through his faith, *Donald Trump* has held total possession for Korean Projects LLC and a 59% stake in Trump Korea LLC in a joint partnership with Daewoo Engineering and Construction Ltd.

In *Indonesia*, the President *Donald Trump* has had enormous plans with *Hary Tanoesoedibjo* with an Indonesian billionaire. *Mr. Hary Tanoesoedibjo* and President *Donald Trump* were working to construct a vast resort and hotel with golf course in the isolated forests of West Java and also new Trump tower on the island of Bali. Then, having a linking with *Donald Trump* and *Tanoesoedibjo* would run for president of Indonesia.

In *Russia*, financial relation has been involving *Donald Trump* since the 2016 presidential election. It is a questionable issue which is raised in the House of Representative in 2018. Robert Mueller's 448-page report on Russian impedance in the 2016 presidential election is discovered clearly. It is not clear to the nation when Trump six trademarks in 2016 have been approved by Russian government. Is it the not the violation of the Emoluments Clause of the Constitution?

In *Philippines*, Trump Tower is the conclusive milestone of the capital city of Philippines Manila. The allowing agreement was very money-spinning for Trump, making between $1 million and $5 million in 2018 as the hotel inaugurated its advertising impetus.

In *India*, The 78-storoid Trump Tower Mumbai is developed by *Lodha Group* and Trump Tower Kolkata, a high-rise hotel that achieved Trump between $100,001 and $1 million last year under a licensing agreement. So, it is said, the Trump Organization desires possibly no other foreign country more than India.

In *Georgia*, quickly following Trump's political winning as the President of the United Nations, there was resuscitated attention over the high-steroid building venture. On January 2017, the Trump Organization hauled out of the task with *Silk Road Group*.

In *China*, on February 2017, American President possessed 77 endorsed Chinese trademarks in his own name. And after one month on March 2017, China allowed initial authorization for another 38 trademarks in a quick move designated as "*peculiar*", "*odd*", "*strange*" by various politicians.

In *Panama*, Trump's first global resort scheme, the Trump Ocean Club International Hotel and Tower, developed into an incredible revenue earner next its 2011 inaugural. Trump revealed rounding up $810,795 to deal with the Panama City property in 2017 and somewhere in the range of $100,001 to $1,000,000 to permit the Trump name.

In *Qatar*, Trump's budgetary declaration makes a list of four organizations that might be identified with planned business interests. Qatar has expended intensely on foreign impact operations, dishing out $18 million in the course of the campaign.

3. Donald Trump's Collusion with Hostile Russia for winning Election

In the beginning 2016 Presidential election, *Trump*'s son was welcome to meet with a Russian government official in regards to *"data that would implicate Hillary and… would be valuable to"* Donald Trump. *Donald Trump Jr.* tour was a piece of Russia and its administration's help for Mr. Trump. But the United States Federal law forbids campaigns from requesting or abiding anything of significant worth from a foreign national. In spite of this prohibition, *Trump Jr., Jared Kushner*, and 2016 Presidential election Campaign

Chairman *Paul Manafort* took part altogether at the meeting.

This connection between the Trump group and numerous Russian nationals brings up issues of whether the campaign helped an unfriendly foreign power's dynamic activity against the United States.

4. Donald Trump's Abuse of Power

I think that the Constitutional clause *"high crimes and misdemeanors"* has been committed by the 45th President *Donald Trump* to pressurize others' states head for investigating against political opponent *Joe Biden* and his Son by the application of abuse of power. The high crime is already committed by exchanging something – give me guilt on Joe Biden and his son, and I'll give you consequently military assistance and aid with your economy – I feel that is positively impeachable offense using abuse of power.

President *Trump* took steps to refuse to give help from Ukraine if its Prime Minister Ukrainian President *Volodymyr Zelenskiy* didn't investigate previous Vice President *Joe Biden* and his Son *Hunter Biden*.

Utilizing taxpayer dollars to control a significant partner against *Russia* and assault a political competitor is a reasonable abuse of presidential power.

Besides, this Trump administration attempted to disguise the informant complaint that exposed this dishonesty and corruption to express and label the government employee who recorded it as divided.

What's more, Trump's choice to pardon and to acquit *Joe Arpaio*, who was indicted for hatred for court in the wake of overlooking a court command that he abandon detaining. It is totally abuse of pardon power added up to a maltreatment of the pardon authority that uncovered his lack of concern to peoples' rights, theory of equality before law, and the separation of powers.

Pardoning this conviction makes conflict with the Fifth Amendment of the U.S. Constitution, which enables the judiciary system to issue and authorize injunctions against government authorities who disobey any personal rights.

The 45th American President *Donald Trump* has so far issued 130 executive orders his first three years of Presidency with most of the abusing of the Presidential authority.

The abuse of power is definitely the sort of offense that considers a high crime and misdemeanor, so this question is very much essential that types of offense should be referred as maltreatment or abuse of power or not. There is nothing more destructive to the structures of governmental system than allowing authorities to abuse power for to pile power. At the point when that is allowed, systems rapidly disintegrate into absolutism or despotism.

5. Advocating Political & Police Violence

Many supporters of *Donald Trump* have completed or undermined demonstrations of violence. But President *Donald Trump* has frequently declined to acknowledge any accountability regarding provoking violence in American societies.

However, a countrywide survey led by *ABC News* has recognized at least 36 criminal cases where *Donald Trump* was provoke in direct association with violent acts, endangering of violence or charges of physical attack.

Figure 4

Donald Trump provoking directly 36 criminal Violence

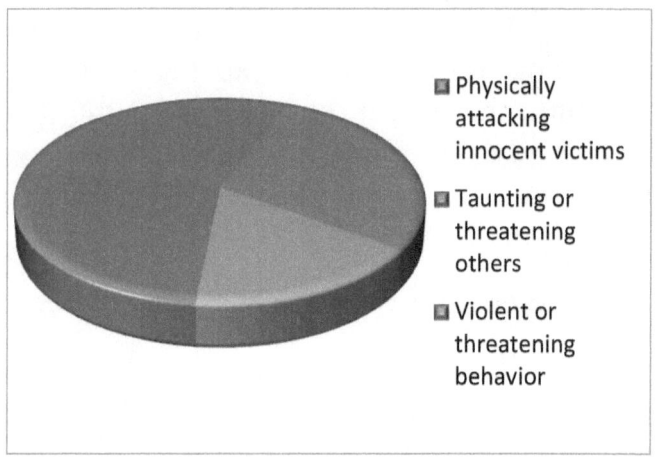

According to the above figure, culprits greeted *Donald Trump* in the taking oath of 2016 President Election of physically assaulting blameless innocent people in 9 cases.

In another 10 cases, Culprits applauded or safeguarded *Donald Trump* while insulting or undermining others. What's more, in another 10 cases, *Donald Trump* and his magniloquence talk were referred to court to clarify a respondent's violent or threatening conduct.

Lastly, in seven cases included brutal violent or undermining acts executed in rebellion of *Donald Trump*.

The above figure chalk out the very sensible horrible factor when we did not find out any of the single criminal case sued in federal court or state court where a demonstration of violence or insulting or physically assaulting was recorded in the name of President Barack Obama or President George W. Bush.

Another statistics of threats or acts of violence committed by Trump supporters (2015-2019) is very much criminalize to *Donald Trump* which is similar to high crime and misdemeanor of Donald Trump.

Figure 5

Threats or acts of violence committed by Trump supporters (2015-2019)

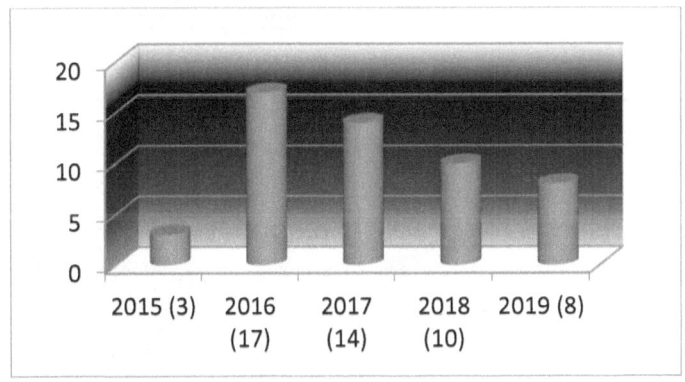

Since Trump started on his campaign for the US presidency run in June 2015, many assaults or threats including his followers have been counted. Here, the Guardian[48] has incorporated 52 cases revealed since 2015 connecting Trump supporters.

When Trump stimulated police officers to abuse publics they have under their custody, he violated his responsibility to administer accurate implementation of the rule of laws. Donald Trump and his oratory supporters have been mentioned in various criminal proceedings as being the encouragement and excuse for political violence.

6. Donald Trump involving in Irresponsible Conduct

Trump can't be allowed to wildly and unnecessarily imperil a huge number of Americans with his insecure conduct. High-positioning federal government authorities engaged with foreign issues have flagged that Trump doesn't have the ability to create learned and wise decisions in the occasion regarding a military emergency. Much more terrible, his activities could start an unnecessary showdown coming from misconception or erroneous conclusion. The whole American understands full impact that *Donald Trump* tweets or creates an open public announcement provoking and

---

[48] Jon Swaine and Juweek Adolphe, "Violence in the name of Trump", the Guardian, Wed 28 Aug 2019

intimidating the North Korean government.

The American President is the *"Commander in Chief of the Army and Navy of the United States"*. But *Donald Trump* as a Commander in Chief of the Army and a Commander in Chief of the Navy, his behavior is completely reckless, careless and malicious that put a large number of lives in danger. If he is unfit to play out his obligations and responsibility as Commander in Chief, *Donald Trump* can't be permitted to stay in the position. So, he should be impeached in that ground.

7. Donald Trump Demolished the Presidential Tradition

Donald Trump is challenging the organization of the presidency not at all like any of his 44 ancestors in Presidency. We have never had a president so evil-educated about the idea of his office, so nakedly and oppressively dishonest, so deleterious egotism, or so shameless in his oppressive obliterate attacks on the courts, the press, the media, the social media, Congress including Republican members, and even senior authorities inside his own government. Trump is a Frankenstein's gigantic monster of former presidents' worst characteristics:

- President *Donald Trump* overcame rage and anger of 7th President Andrew Jackson (1829–

1837). The 45th President *Donald Trump* is demonstrated very much *anger, grudge, malice, annoyance, bother, provocation, nagging, chagrin, humiliation, intolerance, resentment, irritation, mercilessness, antagonism, resentment, harassment, embarrassment, dishonor, shortage of knowledge, oppression, contumelious, and scolding* etc.

- President *Donald Trump* overcame the fanaticism of the 13th President Millard Fillmore (1850–1853). The 45th President *Donald Trump* is demonstrated more *bigotry, fanaticism, zealotry, superstition, extremism, fundamentalism, prejudice, orthodoxy, bias, dedication to his business, conservativeness, adversity, animosity, antipathy, ill will, prejudice, evil, harm, mischief, injury, bale, prejudice, prejudice, and partiality* than Millard Fillmore.

- President *Donald Trump* overcame ineptitude and disdain of the 15th James Buchanan (1857–1861). The 45th President *Donald Trump* is demonstrated more *ineptitude, disdain, stupidity, foolishness, ineptness, ineptitude, crassness, blindness, ineptness, ineptitude, inconsistency, scorn, disregard, peeve, stupidity, foolishness, ineptness, ineptitude, crassness, blindness, ignorance, stupidity, barbarism, foolishness, opaque, opaqueness, obtuseness, thickness, opaqueness, inertia, worldliness, imbecility, inactivity, dull brain, dotage, imbecility, torpor, inertia, stupidity, worldliness, torpor, languor, idiocy, unconsciousness, stupor, mind paralysis, torpidity, languor, ambiguity, obscurity, gloom, illegibility, torpidity, oscitancy, hebetude, insensibility, inertia, stupidity, worldliness, torpor, languor, idiocy, obtuseness, stupidity, opaqueness, insignificancy, and lowliness* etc. than James Buchanan.

- President *Donald Trump* overcame the self-glorification of the 26th President Theodore Roosevelt (1901–1909). The 45th President *Donald Trump* is demonstrated more *self-aggrandizement, self-promotion, self-importance, self-glory, self-important, arrogant, self-glorification, self-celebration, extolment, self-veneration, self-publicity, self-praise, commendation, self-adoration, self-laud, self-accolade, self-eulogy, self-admiration, self-deification, self-applause, self-acclamation, self-commendation and self-flattery* etc. than Theodore Roosevelt.

- President *Donald Trump* overcame distrustfulness, instability, and apathy to law of the 37th President Richard M. Nixon (1969–1974). The 45th President *Donald Trump* is demonstrated more *incredulity, misgiving, distrust, skepticism, astonishment, instability, unpredictability, variability, uncertainty, paranoia, insecurity, unsteadiness, volatility, wobbliness, instability, indifference to law, lethargy to law, ennui to law, dispiritedness to law, unconcern to law, sluggishness to law, apathy to law, and disregard to law* than Richard M. Nixon.

- President *Donald Trump* overcame Bill Clinton's absence of poise, reflexive dishonesty and reflexive unscrupulousness. William J. Clinton (1993–2001) is the 42nd President of the United States. The 45th President *Donald Trump* is demonstrated more absence of poise, lack of dignity, nonexistence of *self-confidence, deficiency of self-control, absenteeism, deficiency of aplomb, reflexive unscrupulousness, spontaneous corruptness, reflexive dishonesty, reflexive immorality, spontaneous ruthlessness, reflexive deceit, voluntary fraudulence, intended deviousness, intentional dishonesty* than Bill Clinton.

Above all the 6 American Presidents who sometimes tried to break down the American democracy by their personal incapacity and personal ill-characteristics. But the 45th President *Donald Trump* has taken power with his evil-intellectuality for demolishing more than 350 years of the American democratic traditions. The basic pillar of the American Constitution's checks and balances theory has principally prevented *Donald Trump* from violating the law to a great extent. And while *Donald Trump* has harmed his own government and his descendants likely won't rehash his pointless tricks. The prediction for the rest of American democratic principles is very *stern, forbidding, dour, formidable, harsh, steely, flinty, stony, churlish, implacable, ruthless, merciless, bleak, dreary, dismal, dingy, wretched, miserable, depressing, cheerless, comfortless, joyless, and gloomy* to implication *rule of law* etc.

However, *Donald Trump*'s strange and peculiar conduct has coarsened legal issues in the political field of America and instigated destructive norm-breaking by the governmental organizations he has mugged.

8. Violating Court Order

Now, the toughest interrogation (?????????????) mark suddenly raised in the heart of all the Americans that how and why the American constitutional law will be the sword of the American citizens in the present situation committed by *Donald Trump*. Why does a president, who regulates what *Alexander Hamilton* depicted as *"the sword of the community,"* maintain a judicial decision President *Donald Trump* dislikes?

But, *Donald Trump* wouldn't have been the first principal president to disobey a court order. A month and a half into the Civil War, Abraham Lincoln opposed a decision by Chief Justice Roger B. Taney that the president came up short on the power to suspend the writ of habeas corpus, and Franklin Roosevelt took steps to disregard the Supreme Court in a World War II case including Nazi saboteurs. Then, judicial authority in the American history was concentrated, solidified, condensed, coagulated, condensed, and solidified the next few decades without any violation of both federal and state court's orders. In spite of the fact that many stressed that Nixon would defy the Supreme Court in 1974 when it ordered him to surrender his implicating tapes to a special prosecutor, Nixon mostly complied by the court order.

Would Trump????????????????????????????????? Simple answer, No! Because, there are a lot of lawsuit is filed involving Donald Trump.

The Constitution of the United Nations doesn't express whether a present sitting president might be accused of wrongdoings. The present explanation at the Department of Justice regarding the matter is that a president may not be prosecuted while in office. But if any person believed the sitting President *Donald Trump* had committed crimes and violated the law, he could make evidence and submit it to Congress to consider impeachment of the President under due process of the United States' Constitution.

A present sitting president of America can't be prosecuted as a person for official activities made while in office, courts have chosen. By *the Jones v. Clinton* case on 1994, it is held by the U.S. Supreme Court that any prosecution federally filed against sitting president which relates just to unofficial or personal behavior. But, the Supreme Court didn't decide in the filing of lawsuit before a state court in this decision. For this reason, two claims in New York State are presently in progress against Trump, and judges in the two cases have concurred so far that they ought to continue.

Further than Trump, a large number of his relatives and handfuls to several business and election campaign partners face investigation. Some are under criminal inquiry. As president, Trump has boundless pardon authority over federal wrongdoings, and could tactically exculpate any person from any criminal punishment, even while a criminal inquiry is in progress.

There are various noteworthy proceedings in the court including United States President *Donald Trump*. But the following proceedings are excluding the name of the sitting president *Donald Trump* by habeas corpus requests:

United States Constitution related Litigations:

President *Donald Trump* has committed offences by the violation of the most important clauses in the U.S. Constitution. He has violated the First Amendment to the U.S. Constitution, the Fifth Amendment to the U.S. Constitution, the Fourteenth Amendment to the U.S. Constitution, and the Foreign Emoluments Clause of the United States Constitution.

For the violation of the First Amendment to the U.S. Constitution, three lawsuits have been filed against *Donald Trump* such as,

Firstly, *Knight First Amendment Institute v. Trump* on July 11, 2017 in the United States District Court for the Southern District of New York for violation of their First Amendment rights and it is decided May 23, 2018;[49]

Secondly, *PEN America v. Trump* is filed July 15, 2019 for violating the First Amendment rights of journalists against President Trump through his threats and it is also utilized government authorities to punish the speech of Trump's media opponents.

Thirdly, **CNN v. Trump** filed on November 13, 2018, in the United States District Court for the District of Columbia for in the infringement of the First Amendment right to freedom of the press and Fifth Amendment right to due process.

For the violation of the Fifth Amendment to the U.S. Constitution, one lawsuit has been filed against *Donald Trump* such as, **New York v. Trump** which is known as the *DACA* (Deferred Action for Childhood Arrivals) lawsuit.

For the violation of the Fourteenth

---

[49] Oprysko, Caitlin (July 9, 2019). "Judges: Trump violates First Amendment when he blocks Twitter critics". Politico. Archived from the original on August 7, 2019. Retrieved July 25, 2019.

Amendment to the U.S. Constitution, only one lawsuit has been filed against *Donald Trump* such as, Stone v. Trump is filed on August 28, 2017 in the United States District Court for the District of Maryland for prohibition on transgender personnel joining the U.S. military. This is the focused infringement transgender personnel's equal protection and due process rights under the Fourteenth Amendment to the U.S. Constitution.

For the violation of the Foreign Emoluments Clause of the United States Constitution, three lawsuits have been filed against *Donald Trump* such as,

Firstly, **CREW (Citizens for Responsibility and Ethics in Washington) v. Trump** is filed on April 18, 2017 before the United States District Court for the Southern District of New York against *Donald Trump* for violation of the Foreign Emoluments Clause by taking gifts or payments from foreign governments.

Secondly, **D.C. and Maryland v. Trump** is filed in the United States District Court for the District of Maryland on June 12, 2017 against President *Donald Trump* for breaking up the Foreign Emoluments Clause of the United States Constitution by receiving gifts from foreign governments.[50]

Thirdly, ***Blumenthal v. Trump*** is filed in the United States District Court for the District of Columbia by the plaintiffs, 30 Senators and 166 Representatives against *Donald Trump* for the violation of the Foreign Emoluments Clause.

Executive Orders related Litigations:

Executive orders are the main sword of the Presidents of the United States to assistance federal government officers and agencies of the executive branch accomplish operations within the government. By the application of the issuing executive orders, current President *Donald Trump* issued total 133 (13765-13897) executive orders from the January 20, 2017 to present by 55 (13765-13819) in 2017, 37 (13820-13856) in 2018, 41 (13857-13897) in 2019. Among of those 133 orders, three Executive Orders including *Executive Order 13768, Executive Order 13769,* and *Executive Order 13780* subject to lawsuits.

The following two prosecutions are filed for sanctuary cities against executive Order 13768:

- ***City and County of San Francisco v. Trump*** is filed in the United States District Court for the Northern District of California

---

[50] LaFrainere, Sharon (June 12, 2017). "Maryland and D.C. Sue Trump Over His Private Businesses". The New York Times. Retrieved August 27, 2019.

grounding that Executive Order 13768 is contradictory to the United States Constitution as if violates the Fifth and Tenth Amendments to the United States Constitution, and also infringes the doctrine on the separation of powers. Executive Order 13768 titled Enhancing Public Safety in the Interior of the United States was issued by U.S. President *Donald Trump* on January 25, 2017.

- **City of Chelsea v. Trump** is filed in the U.S. District Court in Boston on February 8, 2017 with the cities of Chelsea, Massachusetts and Lawrence, Massachusetts challenging the legitimacy of the executive order 13768.

The following seven prosecutions are filed against temporary immigration restrictions executive Order 13769:

- *Aziz v. Trump*
- *Darweesh v. Trump*
- *Doe v. Trump*
- *Louhghalam v. Trump*
- *Mohammed v. United States*
- *Sarsour v. Trump*
- *State of Washington and State of Minnesota v. Trump*

All of the above cases are filed for challenging executive Order 13769 signed by *Donald Trump* on January 27, 2017 for *"Protecting the Nation from Foreign Terrorist Entry into the United States"*.

The following three prosecutions are filed against a revised order on temporary immigration restrictions executive Order 13780:

- *Hawaii v. Trump*, a civil litigation, is filed in the State of Hawaii on March 7, 2017 challenging the executive order 13780, examining for declaratory judgment and an injunction stumbling the order 13780. The plaintiff of this civil litigation complained on eight specific causes of action relating to *Executive Order 13780*.
  ❖ Firstly, the Executive Order 13780 infringed the First Amendment Establishment Clause apply for the travel ban targets Muslims;
  ❖ secondly, the Executive Order 13780 also infringed the Fifth Amendment Equal Protection Clause;
  ❖ thirdly, the Executive Order 13780 infringed also the Fifth Amendment Substantive Due Process clause;
  ❖ fourthly, the Executive Order 13780 also infringed the Fifth Amendment Procedural Due Process clause;
  ❖ fifthly, the Executive Order 13780 also infringed the Immigration and Nationality

Act 8 U.S.C. § 1152(a)(1)(A), 8 U.S.C. § 1182(f) and 8 U.S.C. § 1185(a);
- ❖ sixthly, the Executive Order 13780 also infringed the Religious Freedom Restoration Act 42 U.S.C. § 2000bb1(a);
- ❖ seventhly, the Executive Order 13780 also infringed the Administrative Procedure Act through Violations of the Constitution, *Immigration and Nationality Act*, and Arbitrary and *Capricious Action* 5 U.S.C. § 706(2)(A)–(C); and lastly, *the Executive Order 13780* also infringed the *Administrative Procedure Act* 5 U.S.C. § 706(2)(D), 5 U.S.C. § 551(1), and 5 U.S.C. § 553.
- *International Refugee Assistance Project v. Trump* is argued on 8 May 2017 in the United States Court of Appeals for the Fourth Circuit.

Washington v. Trump is filed on February 7, 2017 in the United States Court of Appeals for the Ninth Circuit challenging the legitimacy and constitutionality of Executive Order which violates Fifth Amendment (*the Due Process Clause - by denying the equal protection of the laws*), Fourteenth Amendment, First Amendment (*the Establishment Clause-by preferring one religion over another*), Fifth Amendment (*right to procedural due process*), *Immigration and Nationality Act*- discriminatory visa procedures, *Immigration and Nationality Act*- the denial of asylum and withholding of removal, *the United Nations Convention against Torture* (ratified by the U.S. in 1994), *Foreign Affairs Reform and Restructuring Act* of 1998, 8 U.S.C. § 1231, *the Religious Freedom Restoration Act*, *the Administrative Procedure Act* (a procedural violation), *Tenth Amendment*, and *the Administrative Procedure Act* (a substantive violation).

Presidential Proclamations related Litigations:

President *Donald Trump* issued a Proclamation on *"Addressing Mass Migration Through the Southern Border of the United States"*, which particularly addressing U.S. Code Title 8. Aliens and Nationality Chapter, 12. Immigration and Nationality, Subchapter II. Immigration Part II. Admission Qualifications for Aliens; Travel Control of Citizens and Aliens Section, 1182. Inadmissible Aliens. It was challenge by a prosecution by four organizations that deliver legal and social services to immigrants and refugees. This case is *"East Bay Sanctuary Covenant v. Trump"* filed on November 9, 2018.

Presidential Memorandums related Litigations:

The following four prosecutions are filed against Presidential Memorandum on Military Service by Transgender Individuals issued by

Donald Trump on August 25, 2017:

- *Jane Doe v. Trump*
- *Stone v. Trump*
- *Karnoski v. Trump*
- *Stockman v. Trump*

Probable legal violations related Litigations:

The violation of different clauses on the Presidential Records Act of 1978, the Federal Advisory Committee Act, and the Dodd–Frank Act of 2010 is categorized as the probable legal violations related Litigations.

Firstly, it is explained that the violation of *the Presidential Records Act of 1978* by filing *CREW* and *National Security Archive v. Trump* and *EOP* case. *CREW* and *National Security Archive v. Trump* and *EOP* is a lawsuit claiming violations of the Presidential Records Act of 1978, 44 U.S.C. §§ 2201–2207. *Citizens for Responsibility and Ethics in Washington (CREW)* and National Security Archive filed a prosecution before the United States District Court for the District of Columbia for infringement of U.S. Code Title 44. Public Printing and Documents, Chapter 22. Presidential Records, Section 2201. Definitions. Specific allegations were President *Donald Trump* removed tweets in violation of the Presidential Records Act of 1981 and the White House utilized encrypted and auto-deleting messaging software which the *Citizens for Responsibility and Ethics in Washington (CREW)* and the *National Security Archive* claims obstructs with other government federal bodies from accomplishing their responsibilities.

Secondly, violation of *the Federal Advisory Committee Act*. The three cases submitted against the establishment of Presidential Advisory Commission on Election Integrity under the Federal Advisory Committee Act. The following three cases are challenged the legitimacy of the establishment of Presidential Advisory Commission on Election Integrity:

- ***ACLU v. Trump and Pence* case:** ACLU v. Trump is a prosecution submitted before the United States District Court for the District of Columbia. The American overseer group American Civil Liberties Union (ACLU) is the plaintiff and President *Donald Trump* and the Vice President Michael Pence are the defendants. The plaintiff has challenged for instituting the Presidential Advisory Commission on Election Integrity for the objectives of supporting the President.
- ***Joyner v. Presidential Advisory Commission on Election Integrity* case:** Joyner v. Presidential Advisory Commission

on Election Integrity is a federal lawsuit filed before the United States District Court for the Southern District of Florida. *Arthenia Joyner*, the *American Civil Liberties Union of Florida*, and others are the plaintiffs. The plaintiffs pursued to instruct the State of Florida from transferring state voter registers to the Presidential Advisory Commission on Election Integrity.

- ***NAACP v. Trump* case:** NAACP Legal Defense & Educational Fund, Inc. v. Trump is a lawsuit pending before the United States District Court for the Southern District of New York. The NAACP Legal Defense Fund, the Ordinary People Society, and a coalition of civil rights groups are the plaintiffs. They are claiming to abuse the Fifth and Fifteenth Amendments and the Federal Advisory Committee Act by founding the Presidential Advisory Commission on Election Integrity (PEIC). The defendants President *Donald Trump*, the Vice President *Michael Pence*, and *Kris Kobach* are deliberately discriminating against Black and Latino voters in abusing of the Fifth and Fifteenth Amendments to the Constitution and the Federal Advisory Committee Act.

Thirdly, violation of the *Dodd–Frank Wall Street Reform* and *Consumer Protection Act, 2010* which is generally known as the *Dodd–Frank Act of 2010*, is a United States federal law that was passed on July 21, 2010. On the scrutinizing of the legality of the appointment of *Mick Mulvaney* as the Acting Director of *the Consumer Financial Protection Bureau (CFPB)*, the aggrieved person *Leandra English* is filed a case against *Donald Trump* and *Mick Mulvaney* violating § 5491(b)(5)(B) of U.S. Code Title 12. Banks and Banking, Chapter 53. Wall Street Reform and Consumer Protection, Subchapter V. Bureau of Consumer Financial Protection, Part A. Bureau of Consumer Financial Protection Section 5491. Establishment of the Bureau of Consumer Financial Protection.

"(5) Deputy Director-There is established the position of Deputy Director, who shall—

(A) be appointed by the Director; and

(B) serve as acting Director in the absence or unavailability of the Director."

English v. Trump case is submitted for the validity of the above § 5491(b)(5)(B).

2020 United States Census related Litigations:

The following two prosecutions are filed against the 2020 United States Census which Census will be the twenty-fourth United States Census.

- Department of Commerce v. New York
- New York Immigration Coalition v. United States Department of Commerce

Trump political campaigns related Litigations:

The following five prosecutions have been filed against *Donald Trump* around 2016 *Donald Trump* political campaigns:

- *Thorne v. Donald J Trump for President Inc.*
- *Democratic National Committee v. Russian Federation (dismissed)*
- *State of NY v. The Trump Foundation*
- *Galicia v. Trump*
- *Nwanguma v. Trump*

Trump potential sexual misconduct and assault related Litigations:

The following five prosecutions have been filed against *Donald Trump* potential sexual misconduct and assault:

- *Katie Johnson v. Donald J Trump and Jeffrey E Epstein*
- *Jane Doe v. Donald Trump & Jeffrey E Epstein*
- *Johnson v. Trump*
- *Zervos v. Trump*
- *Carroll v. Trump*

Trump financial manipulation and employee payment related Litigations:

The following two prosecutions have been filed against *Donald Trump* financial manipulation and employee payment:

- *Cintron v. Trump Organization*
- *Doe et al. v. Trump Corp. et al.*

Trump's financial and tax information related Litigations:

The following three prosecutions have been filed against *Donald Trump* financial and tax information:

- *Trump et al v. Mazars et al*
- *Trump et al v. Deutsche Bank et al*
- *Donald J. Trump v. Committee on Ways and Means, et al.*

Environmental concerns related Litigations:

Juliana, et al. v. United States of America, et al. is an environmental concerns prosecution. It is submitted by twenty one young petitioners against the United States and numerous executive officers including previous President Barack Obama and current President *Donald Trump* in 2015.

9. Oppressing Political Opponents by Donald Trump

The investigation of Mullen echoes that *Donald Trump*'s recurrently stated and communicated wish to oppress his political opponents. He flagged this craving during the election campaign when he commanded serenades of *"lock her up"* against Hillary Clinton, despite the fact that no law disallows utilization of a private email server and an administration investigation found no reason for criminal trial.

President Trump has frequently compelled the Department of Justice and the FBI to investigate and file criminal trial against political opponents like Hillary Clinton; presently, the *Department of Justice (DOJ)* has revived the *Clinton* email examination trying to humiliate his rivals.

This is not grounded in alarming with national security, rule of law, legal implementation, or some other capacity of his office—it is an endeavored by political power play with malice strategic maneuver.

Donald Trump and his political partners have pressurized the Department from Justice (DOJ) to accuse not only Hillary Clinton, but also *James Comey, John Kerry, Mayor Libby Schaaf of Oakland*, and to inquiry *Joe Biden*. *Donald Trump* has also urged prosecuting attorney not to follow

Republicans committing offences, for fear that their criminal accusation harm the Republicans' electoral possibilities.

Democracy protectors in the House of Representatives in Congress also essential an unmistakable, basic message about Trump's thirst power to oppress political rivals, and they must to revise that message following each new occasion of misuse of *Donald Trump*'s authority. While impeachment inquiries against *Donald Trump* would give the perfect discussion to this messaging, political pioneers ought to convey the message as reliably and regularly as they can paying little respect to how they investigate *Donald Trump*'s progressing exertion to destabilize American tradition of democracy.

There's no question that these actions constitute an outrageous and inappropriate abuse of executive branch powers and serve as clear grounds for impeachment.

Doubtlessly that these activities comprise a crazy and inappropriate maltreatment of official branch authorities and serve as a clear, strong and robust reason for impeachment of the President *Donald Trump*.

10. Attacking the Free Press of Donald Trump

A free press and freedom of speech is one of the most important pillars of the United States constitution and also be called basic sword of the United States democracy. The First Amendment of the United States Constitution declares that-

> *"Congress shall make no law respecting an establishment of religion, or prohibiting the free exercise thereof; or abridging the freedom of speech, or of the press, or the right of the people peaceably to assemble, and to petition the Government for a redress of grievances."*

This Constitutional Amendment is the safeguard of free speech and free press in the United States. Only 45 words of the First Amendment of the United States Constitution give the American peoples a great victory against heteronomy of speech by any autocratic government. The First Amendment of the United States Constitution is the security device of American traditional democracy.

But the President *Donald Trump* has frequently criticized the notion of independent press and media as well as freedom of speech. The 'one' twitter message is bearing conclusive evidence of the criticizing the independency of press and media as well as freedom of speech.

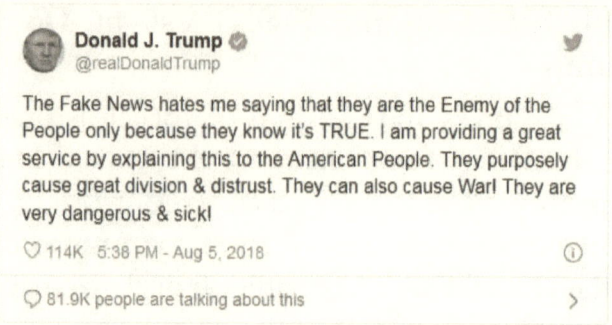

In that message, he is treated the critical reportage of the media as *"fake news"* and who are reporting the news he also treated the journalists as *"the enemy of the American people,"*. By using of such terms President *Donald Trump* blow a punch to the First Amendment of the United States Constitution. He and his Administration of the U.S. government have constantly and falsely revoked press and media authorizations for critical coverage. President *Donald Trump* also seems that the Fake News Media is the primary opponent of him, not the Democrats.

For the repeatedly attacking of Americans great pride in their press freedom and speech freedom, the United States ranks number 43 out of 180 countries on the World Press Freedom Index.

So, this types of continuous activities of attacking and revoking of the press, media and news and President *Donald Trump*'s reluctance to respect and uphold the United Nations' Constitutional Clause on freedom of speech, and contempt for the vital fundamentals to the American free society.

One of the most reliable articles of impeachment of the disordered Trump presidency is the consistent attacks against the press and media to impeach the American 45th President.

Lastly, it is presented all the legal troubles in the Trump era by following figure.

Figure 6
All the Legal Trouble in Trump world[51]

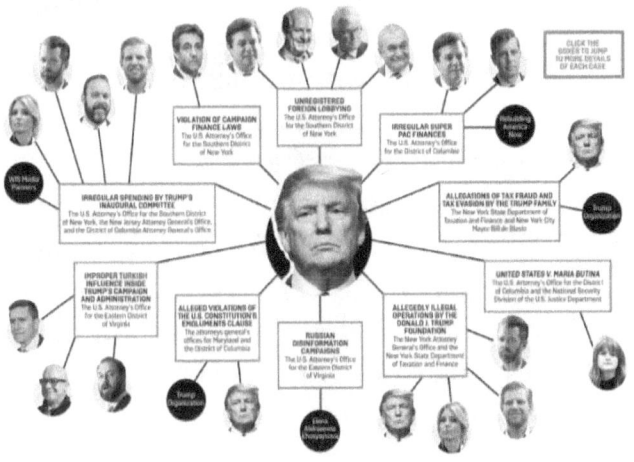

---

[51] Jefcoate O'Donnell, "All the Legal Trouble in Trumpworld", FP, March 8, 2019, Retrieved from https://foreignpolicy.com

Possible Articles of Impeachment against Donald Trump

The following 26 possible Articles of Impeachment against *Donald Trump* may be included in the investigation of the *Donald Trump* Impeachment Case.

1. Infringement of Domestic Emoluments Constitutional Clause
2. Infringement of Foreign Emoluments Constitutional Clause
3. Incitement of Violence
4. Obstruction with Voting Rights by voter intimidation and suppression
5. Discrimination on the Basis on Religion
6. Unlawful War
7. Unlawful Threat of Nuclear War
8. Abuse of Pardon Power
9. Obstruction of Justice
10. Politicizing Prosecutions
11. Plotting Conspiracy Against the United States with a Foreign Government
12. Inability to Rationally Prepare for or Respond to Hurricanes Harvey and Maria
13. Isolating Children and Infants from Families
14. Unlawfully Attempting to Influence the 2016 Election
15. Tax Fraud and Public Misrepresentation

16. Attacking Freedom of the Press
17. Supporting a Revolution in Venezuela
18. Unconstitutional Declaration of Emergency
19. Instructing Border Patrol to Violate the Law
20. Refusal to Comply with Subpoenas
21. Declaration of Emergency Violating the Will of Congress without Basis
22. Unlawful Proliferation of Nuclear Technology
23. Illegitimately Eliminating the United States from the Intermediate-Range Nuclear Forces Treaty
24. Pursuing to Utilize Foreign Governments to Investigate Against Political Rivals
25. Refusal to Comply with Impeachment Inquiry
26. Threatening To Dismantle The Proposition That No Person Is Above The Law

Here, the above 26 possible Articles of Impeachment against *Donald Trump* Impeachment Case are discussed.

1. Infringement of Domestic Emoluments Constitutional Clause

For deciding the first Article of Impeachment of the President of the United States, *Donald J.*

Trump, it is preferred to choose the issue of **'Infringement of Domestic Emoluments Constitutional Clause',** because his personal and official behavior is totally against of the United States Constitutional clause on domestic emoluments.

Article II, Section 1 of the United States Constitution states that *"to take care that the laws be faithfully executed"*.

Above clause given two types of constitutional of the President of the United States:

Firstly, the President of the United States' constitutional oath to loyally perform the office of President of the United States; and

Secondly, the President of the United States could be expected to preserve as a safeguard, to protect as a security guard, and to defend as a defender of the team of the U.S. Government of the Constitution of the United States from any kind of violation of its.

Article I, Section 9, Clause 8 of the United States Constitution is provided by an arrangement for Nobility Clause using the title *"No Title of Nobility shall be granted by the United States"* that forbids the federal government

Article I, Section 9, Clause 8 of the United States Constitution entitled *"No Title of Nobility shall be granted by the United States"* and states that

> *"And no Person holding any Office of Profit or Trust under them, shall, without the Consent of the Congress, accept of any present, Emolument, Office, or Title, of any kind whatever, from any King, Prince, or foreign State."*

It has provided that unlawfully received emoluments, payments, remunerations, rewards, fees, from the United States federal government and from any state governments is the clear violation of Article I, Section 9, Clause 8 of the United States Constitution.

The Constitutional restriction on domestic payments Article I, Section 9, Clause 8 is the reflection of Article II, Section 1 *"to take care that the laws be faithfully executed"* and it is absolutely restricted, not waivable by Congress, and not expose to demonstrating a specific defiling impact.

President Trump's rent of the Old Post Office Building in Washington D.C. disregards the General Services Administration rent contract which expresses:

> *"No ... elected official of the Government of the United States ... shall be admitted to any share or part of this Lease, or to any benefit that may arise therefrom."*

The General Services Administration's inability to authorize that agreement establishes an emolument or a benefit.

President *Donald J. Trump*, have performed a lot of contrary activities in a way in opposition to his faith and belief as a President, and devastating of constitutional government, to the preconception of the reason for law and justice and to show damage of the citizens of the United States.

Wherefore, the 45th President of the United States *Donald J. Trump* is liable of an impeachable offense by such conducts which justifying expulsion from his White House.

2. Infringement of Foreign Emoluments Constitutional Clause

Article I, Section 9, Clause 8 of the United States Constitution is provided by an arrangement for Nobility Clause using the title *"No Title of Nobility shall be granted by the United States"* that forbids the President of America from unlawfully received emoluments, payments, remunerations, rewards, fees, from any foreign governments. It is the clear violation of Article I, Section 9, Clause 8 of the United States Constitution.

Article I, Section 9, Clause 8 of the United

States Constitution entitle *"No Title of Nobility shall be granted by the United States"* and states that

> *"And no Person holding any Office of Profit or Trust under them, shall, without the Consent of the Congress, accept of any present, Emolument, Office, or Title, of any kind whatever, from any King, Prince, or foreign State."*

By the above clause restricts foreign emoluments by the U.S. Constitution (Article I, Section 9).

The current President of America *Donald J. Trump*'s business has permitting manages two Trump Towers in Istanbul, Turkey. And also have created a conflict of interest by the China's state-owned Industrial and Commercial Bank of China and the Embassy of Kuwait, Washington D.C. hotel infringing of the U.S. Constitution on foreign emoluments clause.

In these and numerous comparable activities and choices, President *Donald J. Trump* has acted in a way in opposition to his trust as President, and incendiary of sacred government, to the bias of the reason for law and equity and to show damage of the individuals of the United States. Wherefore, President *Donald J. Trump*, by such direct contrary infringements of the foreign emolument clause of the United States' Constitution, is liable of an impeachable offense justifying expulsion from office.

3. Incitement of Violence

For deciding the third Article of Impeachment of the President of the United States, *Donald J. Trump*, it is preferred to choose the issue of "Incitement of Violence', because his personal behavior on campaigning for election and his present official behavior is completely against of the United States Constitutional responsibility under Article II, Section 1 of the Constitution *"to take care that the laws be faithfully executed,"* has includes wrongfully provoked ferocity inside the United States and illegally driven violence within the United States.

Some specimen of public and open stage speeches as a candidate *Donald J. Trump* on 2016th Election Campaign:

> *"If you see somebody getting ready to throw a tomato, knock the crap out of them. I promise you, I will pay for the legal fees."*
>
> *"You know what I hate? There's a guy, totally disruptive, throwing punches, we're not allowed to punch back anymore. I love the old days—you know what they used to do to guys like that when they were in a place like this? They'd be carried out on a stretcher, folks."*
>
> *"See the first group, I was nice. Oh, take your time. The second group, I was pretty nice. The third*

group, I'll be a little more violent. And the fourth group, I'll say get the hell out of here!"

"I'd like to punch him in the face, I tell ya."

"He was swinging, he was hitting people, and the audience hit back. That's what we need more of."

Various occurrences of viciousness, violence, ferocity, vehemence, forcefulness, aggressiveness, wildness, savagery, and fierceness pursued these and other similar remarks.

President *Donald J. Trump*, have performed a lot of contrary activities in a way in opposition to his faith and belief as a President, and devastating of legitimate government, to create misconception in the highest post of the powerful states, to destabilize law and justice and to show his viciousness, violence, ferocity, vehemence, forcefulness, aggressiveness, wildness, savagery, and fierceness to the citizens of the United States.

Wherefore, the 45th President of the United States *Donald J. Trump* is liable of an impeachable offense by such conducts for removal from his office.

4. Obstruction with Voting Rights by voter intimidation and suppression

For determining the fourth Article of

Impeachment of the President of the United States, *Donald J. Trump*, it is preferred to indicate the issue of "*Obstruction with Voting Rights*', as an impeachable offense of the President *Donald J. Trump* because his personal behavior and activities creates voter intimidation and suppression to the American and his present official behavior is completely against of the United States Constitutional responsibility under Article II, Section 1 of the Constitution *"to take care that the laws be faithfully executed,"* has occupied with demonstrations of voter terrorizing and concealment within the United States.

Since the November 2016 elections to till today, *Donald J. Trump* openly allowed his supporters, to take part in brutishness and violence, to patrol voting places looking for members in practice of voter fraud. His comments included:

> *"I hope you people can sort of not just vote on the 8th, go around and look and watch other polling places, and make sure that it's 100 percent fine."*

> *"We're going to watch Pennsylvania. Go down to certain areas and watch and study and make sure other people don't come in and vote five times."*

Trump asked supporters to target Philadelphia, St. Louis, and different urban communities with enormous minority populaces.

At the point when early casting a ballot started, occurrences were happened for of Trump supporters snapping voters and otherwise frightening them.

After taking the oath as the President, *Donald J. Trump* has proceeded with voter terrorizing endeavors. He has made a Presidential Advisory Commission on Election Integrity, which has sent letters to states mentioning sensitive voter data. Most of the states have declined this request.

President *Donald J. Trump*, have done a lot of conflicting activities using a specific manner opposing to his trust and belief as a President, and subversive of reasonable governmental functioning, to make fallacy in the highest post of the powerful states, to destabilize law and justice and to show the manifest wound of the people of the United States.

Wherefore, the 45th President of the United States *Donald J. Trump* is responsible of an impeachable offense for removal from his office by creating tremendous voter intimidation and suppression to the American.

5. Discrimination on the Basis on Religion

For determining the fifth Article of

Impeachment of the President of the United States, *Donald J. Trump*, it is chosen to specify the issue of *"Discrimination on the Basis on Religion'*, as an impeachable offense of the President *Donald J. Trump* because his personal behavior and activities has proof of engagement of discrimination in infringement of the First Amendment of the United States Constitution and other laws by pursuing to embargo Muslims from entering the United States and his present official behavior is completely against of the United States Constitutional responsibility under Article II, Section 1 of the Constitution *"to take care that the laws be faithfully executed,"* has occupied with demonstrations of segregation disregarding the First Amendment and different laws by looking to forbid Muslims from entering the United States.

Donald J. Trump issued an executive order 13769 on January 27, 2017 Muslim ban on travel to the United States for citizens of Iran, Iraq, Libya, Somalia, Sudan, Syria, and Yemen. This is the first executive order which clearly violates the religious equality and religious freedom of the United States which enumerated of the Free Exercise Clause of the First Amendment states that

> *"Congress shall make no law respecting an establishment of religion, or prohibiting the free*

exercise thereof".

President *Donald J. Trump*, have done numerous contradictory actions by means of opposing to his trust and belief as a President. This violation of Religious Freedom Clause of the First Amendment is subversive of governmental functioning and to make fallacy in the highest post of the powerful states, to weaken law and justice and to show the obvious twisted of the people of the United States.

Wherefore, the 45th President of the United States *Donald J. Trump* is guilty of an impeachable offense for removal from his office banning Muslims entering into the United States creating a division and discrimination on the basic of religion.

6. Unlawful War

For determining the sixth Article of Impeachment of the President of the United States, *Donald J. Trump*, it is favored to point out the issue of '*Unlawful War*', as an impeachable offense of the President *Donald J. Trump* because his personal behavior and activities creates unlawful war against different nations and his present official actions is completely against of the United States Constitutional responsibility under Article II, Section 1 of the Constitution *"to take care that the laws be faithfully executed,"* has pursued various wars disregarding the United Nations Charter and of the Kellogg-Briand Pact, those two treaties are the main basic principles of the declaring war of the United States under Article VI, Clause 2 of the U.S. Constitution.

Article VI, Clause 2 of the U.S. Constitution states that

> *"This Constitution, and the Laws of the United States which shall be made in Pursuance thereof; and all Treaties made, or which shall be made, under the Authority of the United States, shall be the supreme Law of the Land; and the Judges in every State shall be bound thereby, any Thing in the Constitution or Laws of any State to the Contrary notwithstanding."*

President *Donald J. Trump* and his subordinates federal officials endeavored to deceive the United States to the people and Congress about legitimizations for wars, including by professing to have information that the Syrian government utilized chemical weapons, and just as by erroneously expressing the quantity of U.S. troops deployed to different wars.

President Trump has raised bombing operations in Iraq and Syria, bringing about huge quantities of non-military personnel deaths. In the wake of campaigning for office contrary to the war on Afghanistan, Trump has absolutely made it a perpetual operation. President Trump talked at the home office of the Central Intelligence Agency on January 23, 2017, and advanced an illicit strategy of pursuing battles for the stealing of assets. Trump has directed the U.S. military's collaboration in the unlawful bombing of Yemen by Saudi Arabia, disregarding the Leahy Law and bringing about an extreme humanitarian calamity.

President *Donald J. Trump*, have done numerous infringements by conflicting to his trust and belief as a President. This type of violation of war principles Clause of the Article VI, Clause 2 is subversive of governmental functioning and to make fallacy in the highest post of the powerful states, to weaken law and justice and to show the obvious twisted of the people of the United States.

Wherefore, the 45th President of the United States *Donald J. Trump* is guilty of an impeachable offense for removal from his office for U.S. military's collaboration in the unlawful war.

7. Unlawful Threat of Nuclear War

For determining the seventh Article of Impeachment of the President of the United States, *Donald J. Trump*, it is preferred to specify the issue of '*Unlawful Threat of Nuclear War*', as an impeachable offense of the President *Donald J.*

Trump because his personal behavior and activities creates unlawful threat of nuclear war and his present official arrangements is completely against of the United States Constitutional responsibility under Article II, Section 1 of the Constitution *"to take care that the laws be faithfully executed,"* has obviously endangered nuclear war (*"fire and fury"*) against North Korea. This type of endangering of the nuclear war is the proper violation of the United Nations Charter, a treaty that is piece of the Supreme Law of the United States under Article VI, Clause 2 of the U.S. Constitution.

Article VI, Clause 2 of the U.S. Constitution states that

> *"This Constitution, and the Laws of the United States which shall be made in Pursuance thereof; and all Treaties made, or which shall be made, under the Authority of the United States, shall be the supreme Law of the Land; and the Judges in every State shall be bound thereby, any Thing in the Constitution or Laws of any State to the Contrary notwithstanding."*

Again, President *Donald J. Trump* endangered Iran with inviting nuclear war and also announcing an intimidating message-

> *"If Iran needs to battle, that will be the official finish of Iran."*

President *Donald J. Trump*, have done numerous declaring with threat, intimidation, warning of nuclear war which is conflicting to his trust and belief as a President. This type of endangering nuclear war is the gross violation of the Treaty on the Prohibition of Nuclear Weapons (TPNW). The violation of the nuclear war principles also crosses the limit of the Article VI, Clause 2 of the United States. This type of violation is subversive of U.S. governmental functioning and to make fallacy in the highest post of the powerful states, to weaken law and justice and to show the deep twisted of the people of the United States.

Wherefore, the 45th President of the United States *Donald J. Trump* is guilty of an impeachable offense for removal from his office for the nuclear war principles.

8. Abuse of Pardon Power

For determining the eighth Article of Impeachment of the President of the United States, *Donald J. Trump*, it is chosen to state the issue of *'Abuse of Pardon Power'*, as an impeachable offense of the President *Donald J. Trump* because his personal behavior and activities on implementing the pardoning power.

Article II, Section 1 of the United States Constitution states that *"to take care that the laws be faithfully executed*".

Above clause given two types of constitutional of the President of the United States:

Firstly, the President of the United States' constitutional oath to loyally perform the office of President of the United States; and

Secondly, the President of the United States could be expected to preserve as a safeguard, to protect as a security guard, and to defend as a defender of the team of the U.S. Government of the Constitution of the United States from any kind of violation of its.

The present official measures of the President *Donald J. Trump* are completely against of the United States Constitutional responsibility under Article II, Section 1 of the Constitution. He has issued a pardon for former sheriff of *Maricopa County, Arizona, Joe Arpaio*, who had been imprisoned of disdain for inability to conform to a court order in a case accusing him with racial discrimination.

And, President *Donald J. Trump* has guided his subordinates' federal officials to illicitly hold onto private land and infringe environmental laws for to construct a partition wall on the Mexican border line. President *Donald J. Trump* not only directed for the violating the environmental laws but also promised to pardon all the crimes committed by constructing Mexican border.

President *Donald J. Trump*, have done numerous infringements by conflicting to his trust and belief as a President. This type of contrary direction inspires peoples for commission of the crime which is subversive of governmental functioning and to make fallacy in the highest post of the powerful states, to weaken law and justice and to show the obvious twisted of the people of the United States.

Wherefore, the 45th President of the United States *Donald J. Trump* is guilty of an impeachable offense for removal from his office for abusing pardon power and illegal direction to break down laws to make a wall inside Mexico border.

9. Obstruction of Justice

For determining the ninth Article of Impeachment of the President of the United States, *Donald J. Trump*, it is preferred to specify the issue of '*Obstruction of Justice*', as an impeachable offense of the President *Donald J. Trump* because his personal behavior and activities creates unlawful threat of nuclear war and his present official arrangements is completely against of the United States Constitutional responsibility under Article II, Section 1 of the Constitution *"to take care that the laws be faithfully executed,"* has obviously impediment of justice.

Robert Mueller's report encompasses 10 examples of impediment of justice where President *Donald J. Trump* possibly committed obstruction of justice.

In the United States Criminal Justice System, obstruction of justice is a crime consisting of under U.S. Code, Title 18. Crimes and Criminal Procedure, Part I. Crimes, Chapter 73. Obstruction Of Justice (§ 1501-§ 1521) including Assault on process server, Resistance to extradition agent, Influencing or injuring officer or juror generally, Influencing juror by writing, Obstruction of proceedings before departments, agencies, and committees, Theft or alteration of record or process; false bail, Picketing or parading, Recording, listening to, or observing proceedings of grand or petit juries while deliberating or voting, Obstruction of court orders, Obstruction of criminal investigations, Obstruction of State or local law enforcement, Tampering with a witness, victim, or an informant, Retaliating against a witness, victim, or an informant, Civil action to restrain harassment of a victim or witness, Civil action to protect against retaliation in fraud cases, Definitions for certain provisions; general provision,

Obstruction of Federal audit, Obstructing examination of financial institution, Obstruction of criminal investigations of health care offenses, Destruction, alteration, or falsification of records in Federal investigations and bankruptcy, Destruction of corporate audit records, and Retaliating against a Federal judge or Federal law enforcement officer by false claim or slander of title.

From above list of U.S. Code 18, Chapter 73. Obstruction Of Justice (§ 1501-§ 1521), the President *Donald J. Trump* potentially committed obstruction of justice under section § 1505. Obstruction of proceedings before departments, agencies, and committees and § 1510. Obstruction of criminal investigations.

U.S. Code 18, Chapter 73. Obstruction Of Justice, § 1505 entitled *"Obstruction of proceedings before departments, agencies, and committees"* states that

> *"Whoever corruptly, or by threats or force, or by any threatening letter or communication influences, obstructs, or impedes or endeavors to influence, obstruct, or impede the due and proper administration of the law under which any pending proceeding is being had before any department or agency of the United States, or the due and proper exercise of the power of inquiry under which any inquiry or investigation is being had by either House,*

or any committee of either House or any joint committee of the Congress—

Shall be fined under this title, imprisoned not more than 5 years or, if the offense involves international or domestic terrorism (as defined in section 2331), imprisoned not more than 8 years, or both."

U.S. Code 18, Chapter 73. Obstruction Of Justice, § 1510 entitled *"Obstruction of criminal investigations"* states that

"(a) Whoever willfully endeavors by means of bribery to obstruct, delay, or prevent the communication of information relating to a violation of any criminal statute of the United States by any person to a criminal investigator shall be fined under this title, or imprisoned not more than five years, or both."

President *Donald J. Trump* has done numerous violations contradictory to his trust and belief as a President. This type of obstructing prosecutors, investigators, or other government officials which is subversive of governmental functioning and to make fallacy in the highest post of the powerful states, to weaken law and justice and to the show the obvious twisted of the people of the United States.

Wherefore, the 45th President of the United States *Donald J. Trump* is guilty of an impeachable offense for removal from his office for obstructing prosecutors, investigators, or other government officials and Obstruction of criminal investigations under U.S. Code 18, Chapter 73-Obstruction Of Justice.

10. Politicizing Prosecutions

For determining the tenth Article of Impeachment of the President of the United States, *Donald J. Trump*, it is preferred to specify the issue of *'Politicizing Prosecutions'*, as an impeachable offense of the President *Donald J. Trump* because his personal behavior and activities proves politicizing prosecutions and his present official arrangements is completely against of the United States Constitutional responsibility under Article II, Section 1 of the Constitution *"to take care that the laws be faithfully executed,"* has coordinated or tried to direct law enforcement, including the Department of Justice (DoJ) and the Federal Bureau of Investigation (FoB), to investigate and accuse political opponents, foes and others - and to not accuse political partners - for inappropriate purposes not legitimized by any legal activity of his office, in this way disintegrating the standard of law, destabilizing the freedom of law enforcement from legislative issues, politics, and compromising the constitutional right to due process of law.

Since the Presidential Election 2016, the President *Donald J. Trump* is giving pressure the *U.S. Department of Justice (DoJ)* to investigate another President candidate Hillary Clinton, key leaders of the Democratic Party, and other political opponents.

A chief executive, the President of the United States, *Donald J. Trump* who utilizes law enforcement to harass political opponents is the features for a chaotic banana republic, not an established constitutional republic. That is the reason all Republican and Democratic presidents could be expected to respect the impartiality of law enforcement.

But some occurrences for the violation of the independence of law enforcement principles have been committed by the existing 45th the President of the United States *Donald J. Trump*. The violation of the independence of law enforcement principles is treated as *"the greatest danger of abuse of prosecuting power"* by Attorney General (later Supreme Court Justice) Robert Jackson in 1940.

The U.S. Congress set an example with the second article of indictment against President Richard Nixon, which referred to his utilization of government investigative departments against political adversaries. Following this point of reference, the president's endeavors to engage the criminal investigative forces of the federal government against political adversaries for purposes irrelevant to national security, national integrity, the enforcement of laws, or some other legal capacity of his office are reason for impeachment, regardless of whether they didn't overcome in manipulating law enforcement.

President *Donald J. Trump* has done numerous violations contradictory to his trust and belief as a President in the perspective of undue influence of criminal prosecutions, criminal investigations against his political opponents which is subversive of governmental functioning and to make fallacy in the highest post of the powerful states, to weaken the criminal justice system and to the show the noticeable abnormally to the people of the United States.

Wherefore, the 45th President of the United States *Donald J. Trump* is guilty of an impeachable offense for removal from his office for politicizing American traditional criminal justice system by pressuring federal prosecutors, investigators, or other government officials to accuse political opponents.

11. Plotting Conspiracy Against the United States with a Foreign Government

For determining the eleventh Article of Impeachment of the President of the United States, *Donald J. Trump*, it is chosen to specify the issue of '*Plotting Conspiracy Against the United States with a Foreign Government*', as an impeachable offense of the President *Donald J. Trump* because his personal behavior and activities proves that his progress group campaigned foreign governments, including those of Egypt and Russia in the interest of the administration of Israel and his present official arrangements is completely against of the United States Constitutional responsibility under Article II, Section 1 of the Constitution *"to take care that the laws be faithfully executed,"* has collaborated conspiracy against the United States with *Paul Manafort*, Former *Donald J. Trump* Election campaign chairman, was sentenced to 73 months in prison after pleading guilty to two charges in DC District Court.

The President of the United States *Donald J. Trump*'s every drive runs fortified the postwar international system by plotting conspiracy against the United States with a foreign government. All over the world has been observing the death of the U.S.-led liberal order since *Donald J. Trump* era.

The United States and other world were appeared to stand shoulder to shoulder to defend the advances obtained from 70 years of cooperation including international trade, alliances, treaties, pacts, international law, multilateralism, environmental protection, torture, human rights and humanitarian laws—on all these fundamental issues. And now the President of the United States *Donald J. Trump* has instigated to sabotage the order it created since 70 years.

President *Donald J. Trump* has done several defilements contradictory to his trust and belief as a President. This type of plotting conspiracy against the United States with a foreign government which is subversive of governmental functioning and to make fallacy in the highest post of the powerful states, to weaken law and justice and to the show the obvious twisted of the people of the United States.

Wherefore, the 45th President of the United States *Donald J. Trump* is guilty of an impeachable offense for removal from his office for plotting conspiracy against the United States with a foreign government.

12. Inability to Rationally Prepare for or Respond to Hurricanes Harvey and Maria

For determining the twelfth Article of Impeachment of the President of the United States, *Donald J. Trump*, it is selected to specify the issue of **'*inability to rationally prepare for or respond to hurricanes Harvey and Maria*',** as an impeachable offense of the President *Donald J. Trump* because his personal behavior and activities proves that he shows inability of the states without any reasonable excuse during hurricanes Harvey and Maria and his present official response during hurricanes Harvey and Maria is completely against of the United States Constitutional responsibility under Article II, Section 1 of the Constitution *"to take care that the laws be faithfully executed,"* has neglected to sensibly get ready for occasions like Hurricane Harvey and Hurricane Maria or to satisfactorily react to those tropical hurricanes.

The President of the United States *Donald J. Trump*'s responsibility during the hurricanes Harvey and Maria is totally questionable in order to appointment of the new chief director in the vacant post of the Federal Emergency Management Agency (FEMA) until June 2017. His irresponsibility proves the reluctance of the doing better for the most powerful states' people life protector. Another example is not appointing a chief in the National Hurricane Center during Hurricane Harvey in August from May 2017. Even President *Donald Trump* didn't take part in salvage and recuperation tasks during Hurricane Harvey hit the America. And in spite of extensive damage, deficiency of power and electricity, and lack of primary medical care and more than 4,600 people death President Trump declined vital aid when Hurricane Maria smash Puerto Rico in September 2017.

The President of the United States *Donald J. Trump* also signed an executive order dismissing the Federal Flood Risk Management Standard on August 15, 2017. He previously had parted the Advisory Committee for the Sustained National Climate Assessment, and pulled back the United States from the Paris climate agreement.

President *Donald J. Trump* has done several defilements contradictory to his trust and belief as a President. This type of inability to rationally prepare for or respond to hurricanes Harvey and Maria that is subversive of governmental functioning and to make fallacy in the highest post of the powerful states, to weaken law and justice and to show the obvious twisted of the people of the United States.

Wherefore, the 45th President of the United States *Donald J. Trump* is guilty of an impeachable offense for removal from his office for inability to judiciously prepare for or respond to hurricanes Harvey and Maria.

13. Isolating Children and Infants from Families

For determining the thirtieth Article of Impeachment of the President of the United States, *Donald J. Trump*, it is selected to specify the issue of **'isolating children and infants from families'**, as an impeachable offense of the President *Donald J. Trump* because his personal behavior and activities on isolating children and infants from families and his present official forceful action to separate thousands of refugee children and infants from their families is completely against of the United States Constitutional responsibility under Article II, Section 1 of the Constitution *"to take care that the laws be faithfully executed,"* has directed the inhuman order to his subordinates who have coercively isolated a large number of refugee kids and babies from their families, detained them in inhumane conditions.

In these activities, *Donald J. Trump* has mishandled his high office and abused various legitimate prerequisites in an express action to punish and deter individuals who are totally innocent and in other cases *Donald J. Trump* accused of a misdemeanor.

President *Donald J. Trump* has done several defilements contradictory to his trust and belief as a President. This type of isolating children and infants from families that is subversive of governmental functioning and to make fallacy in the highest post of the powerful states, to weaken law and justice and to show the obvious twisted of the people of the United States. These dangerous activities by President Trump have infringed the Universal Declaration of Human Rights, the Convention on the Rights of the Child, the Eighth Amendment to the U.S. Constitution, and the Due Process law of the Fifth Amendment to the U.S. Constitution.

The *Fifth Amendment* to the U.S. Constitution states that-

> *"No person shall be held to answer for a capital, or otherwise infamous crime, unless on a presentment or indictment of a Grand Jury, except in cases arising in the land or naval forces, or in the Militia, when in actual service in time of War or public danger; nor shall any person be subject for the same offence to be twice put in jeopardy of life or limb; nor shall be compelled in any criminal case to be a witness against himself, nor be deprived of life, liberty, or property, without due process of law; nor*

shall private property be taken for public use, without just compensation."

Wherefore, the 45th President of the United States *Donald J. Trump* is guilty of an impeachable offense for removal from his office for interference the attention of guardians in the maintenance, guardianship, custody, safekeeping, and controls of their kids along with violation of the notable the significant liberty interests known by the Court. These activities and orders of the President *Donald J. Trump* has acted conflicting to the tradition of law and justice and to the obvious harm of the citizen of the United States and those people of other countries pursuing asylum and refuge in the United States.

14. Unlawfully Attempting to Influence the 2016 Election

For determining the fourteenth Article of Impeachment of the President of the United States, *Donald J. Trump*, it is selected to specify the issue of **'unlawfully attempting to influence the 2016 election'**, as an impeachable offense of the President *Donald J. Trump* because his personal behavior and activities by illegally attempting to influence the 2016 presidential election is entirely against of the United States Constitutional accountability under Article II, Section 1 of the Constitution *"to take care that the* *laws be faithfully executed,"* has involved in a criminal conspiracy scheme to acquisition the silence of American citizens, and did so with the intent of influencing the election and in violation of campaign finance laws. For that maltreatment to the voters, he did manipulating the political election with the full intention and infringing upon election campaign finance laws.

Cohen confessed illegally attempting to influence the 2016 presidential election in federal court by the following language *"in coordination with and at the direction of a candidate for federal office"* and *"for the principal purpose of influencing the election"* on August 21, 2018.

This evidence entangles *Donald J. Trump* in the offense of collaborating to make an undue and illegitimate 2016 presidential election campaign influence. It also involves him in the high crime and misdemeanor of endeavoring to deceptively influence -- and potentially effectively impact -- the outcome of the 2016th United States presidential election. As President, *Donald J. Trump* said misleadingly false covering the original fact on the election campaign facts and attempted to conceal his crime.

President *Donald J. Trump* has done several defilements contradictory to his trust and belief as a President. Attempting to influence the 2016 presidential election illegally is subversive to the governmental general functioning and to make misconception in the highest post of the powerful states, to weaken law and justice and to show the obvious twisted of the people of the United States.

Wherefore, the 45th President of the United States *Donald J. Trump* is guilty of an impeachable offense for removal from his office for undue influencing the 2016 presidential election.

15. Tax Fraud and Public Misrepresentation

For determining the fifteenth Article of Impeachment of the President of the United States, *Donald J. Trump*, it is selected to specify the issue of **'tax fraud and public misrepresentation',** as an impeachable offense of the President *Donald J. Trump* because his personal behavior and activities demonstrate tax fraud and public misrepresentation and he involved in widespread tax fraud which assisted as the base for his dramatic falsification to the public of his achievements is completely against of the United States Constitutional responsibility under Article II, Section 1 of the Constitution *"to take care that the laws be faithfully executed,"* has committed crime for violating election campaign laws.

President *Donald J. Trump* has done several violations contradictory to his trust and belief as a President. Violation of tax related laws after taking oath as the highest post as president is subversive of governmental functioning and to make fallacy in the highest post of the powerful states, to weaken law and justice and to show the obvious twisted of the people of the United States.

Wherefore, the 45th President of the United States *Donald J. Trump* is guilty of an impeachable offense for removal from his office for violating tax laws and fraudulent activities on revenue.

16. Attacking Freedom of the Press

For determining the sixteenth Article of Impeachment of the President of the United States, *Donald J. Trump*, it is selected to specify the issue of **'*Attacking Freedom of the Press*'**, as an impeachable offense of the President *Donald J. Trump* because his personal behavior and activities prove attacking freedom of the press occurrences and he involved in undermining the freedom of the press is completely against of the United States Constitutional responsibility under Article II, Section 1 of the Constitution *"to take care that the laws be faithfully executed,"* has constantly destabilized the independence of the press and media.

A independence press and media as well as freedom of speech is one of the most significant pillars of the United States constitution and also be called rudimentary weapon of the United States social equality on democratic political government. The First Amendment of the United States' Constitution states that-

> *"Congress shall make no law respecting an establishment of religion, or prohibiting the free exercise thereof; or abridging the freedom of speech, or of the press, or the right of the people peaceably to assemble, and to petition the Government for a redress of grievances."*

This Constitutional Amendment is the safeguard of free speech and free press in the United States. Only 45 words of the First Amendment of the United States Constitution provide a great victory to the American people against heteronomy of speech by any dictatorial government. The First Amendment of the United States Constitution is the safety device of American modern democracy.

But the 45th President *Donald J. Trump* has often condemned the conception of independent press and media as well as freedom of speech. His 'one' twitter note is a conclusive evidence of the criticizing the independency of press and media as well as freedom of speech.

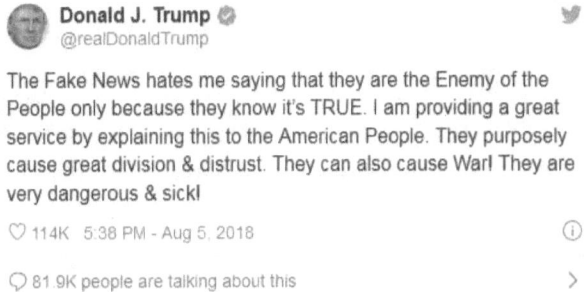

In the above message, he criticized the reportage of the media as *"fake news"* and who are reporting the news he also treated the journalists as *"the enemy of the American people"*. By using of such terms President *Donald Trump* blow a punch to the First Amendment of the United States Constitution. He and his Administration of the U.S. government have frequently and dishonestly revoked press and media owners for critical coverage. President *Donald Trump* also conceptualizes that the Fake News Media is the main opponent of him, not the political opponent, the Democrats.

For the regularly confronting of Americans prodigious pride in their press freedom and speech freedom, the United States ranking stands 43 out of 180 countries on the World Press Freedom Index.

So, this types of nonstop doings of criticizing

and revoking of the press, media and news and President *Donald Trump*'s unwillingness to respect and uphold the United Nations' Constitutional Clause on freedom of speech, and disrespect for the dynamic fundamentals to the American free people.

One of the most reliable articles of impeachment of the disordered Trump presidency is the consistent attacks against the press and media to impeach the American 45th President.

President *Donald J. Trump* has done several abuses contradictory to his trust and belief as a President. Attacking continuously against the independence of press and media is subversive to the governmental general functioning and to make misconception in the highest post of the powerful states, to weaken law and justice and to show the obvious twisted of the people of the United States.

Wherefore, the 45th President of the United States *Donald J. Trump* is guilty of an impeachable offense for removal from his office for criticizing and revoking of the freedom press, media and news.

17. Supporting a Revolution in Venezuela

For determining the seventeenth Article of Impeachment of the President of the United States, *Donald J. Trump*, it is selected to specify the issue of **'Supporting a Revolution in Venezuela',** as an impeachable offense of the President *Donald J. Trump* because his personal behavior and activities prove that they provide support a coup in Venezuela and he involved to organize the revolution in Venezuela which is completely contrary to the United States Constitutional responsibility under Article II, Section 1 of the Constitution *"to take care that the laws be faithfully executed,"* has provided support to occur a revolution in Venezuela.

And also his government's second man, Vice President of the United States Michael Richard Pence, infringes of his promise to reliably accomplish the office of Vice President of the United States and to help and protect the Constitution of the United States, have harmed the standard of law and threatened universal security by supporting a coup endeavor in Venezuela.

On the night of January 22, 2019, after long periods of destructive United States sanctions against Venezuela, which pursued an ineffective 2002 U.S.- bolstered coup endeavor, Vice

President Pence supposedly called *Juan Guaidó* and disclosed to him that the United States would support him if he takes the control in Venezuela. The following day, January 23, *Guaidó* endeavored to do as directed by Pence. And President *Donald J. Trump* gave an announcement perceiving *Guaidó* as the President of Venezuela, in spite of the fact that Venezuela had a elected president. On January 24, 2019, the Trump-Pence organization endeavored ineffectively to convince the Organization of American States to perceive *Guaidó* as president.

President *Donald J. Trump* and Vice President *Michael Richard Pence* have done several misapplications of laws contradictory to their trust and belief as a President and Vice-President. To provide support of a coup in Venezuela is subversive to the governmental general functioning and to make misconception in the highest post of the powerful states, to weaken law and justice and to show the obvious twisted of the people of the United States.

Wherefore, the 45th President of the United States *Donald J. Trump* and Michael Richard Pence is guilty of an impeachable offense for removal from his office for supporting a revolution in Venezuela.

18. Unconstitutional Declaration of Emergency

For determining the eighteenth Article of Impeachment of the President of the United States, *Donald J. Trump*, it is selected to specify the issue of **'Unconstitutional Declaration of Emergency',** as an impeachable offense of the President *Donald J. Trump* because his personal behavior and activities prove that he declares illegal national emergency and he done an anarchic act, a gross misuse of the authority of the presidency and a anxious endeavor to distract from the fact that President Trump violated his basic promise to have Mexico pay for his wall which is completely contrary to the United States Constitutional responsibility under Article II, Section 1 of the Constitution *"to take care that the laws be faithfully executed,"* has proclaimed a national emergency, without any real crisis, for the determination of spending budget on a Mexico border wall that had been assumed for different commitments.

Trump's declaration of a national emergency on construction a wall on Mexico border was criticized by Democrats as unconstitutional including the United States Speaker of the House of Representatives Nancy Pelosi and Senate Minority Leader Chuck Schumer.

By declaration of a national emergency, President Trump has disregarded Article 1, Section 7 of the United States Constitution:

> *"All Bills for raising Revenue shall originate in the House of Representatives; but the Senate may propose or concur with Amendments as on other Bills."*

By declaration of a national emergency, President Trump has also disregarded Article 1, Section 9 of the United States Constitution:

> *"No Money shall be drawn from the Treasury, but in Consequence of Appropriations made by Law; and a regular Statement and Account of the Receipts and Expenditure."*

By declaration of a national emergency, President Trump has also ignored the Federal Anti-Deficiency Statute. By utilizing the United States military to authorize immigration law, President *Donald Trump*'s declared strategy would also infringe *the Posse Comitatus Act 1878*.

Moreover, President J. Trump has manhandled his authority by openly advancing this activity utilizing a progression of lies empowering trepidation, fanaticism, fear, bigotry, hatred, anxiety, racism, animosity, panic, narrow-mindedness, loathing, and scorn. He has dishonestly proposed that immigrants carry out offenses at a higher rate than non-immigrants, that unlawful border crossings have been growing recently, that terrorist and extremist groups have sent agents to enter the United States through Mexico, and that applying for refuge is a frightening or criminal activity.

President *Donald J. Trump* has done several misapplications of laws contradictory to their trust and belief as a President. To promulgate national emergency to collect money for making Mexico wall is subversive to the governmental general functioning and to make misconception in the highest post of the powerful states, to weaken law and justice and to show the obvious twisted of the people of the United States.

Wherefore, the 45th President of the United States *Donald J. Trump* and Michael Richard Pence is guilty of an impeachable offense for removal from his office for issuing illegal declaration of national emergency to collect money for making Mexico wall.

19. Instructing Border Patrol to Violate the Law

For determining the nineteenth Article of Impeachment of the President of the United States, *Donald J. Trump*, it is selected to specify the issue of ***'Instructing Border Patrol to Violate the Law'***, as an impeachable offense of the President *Donald J. Trump* because his personal behavior and instruction to border patrol to violate the law which is completely contrary to the United States Constitutional responsibility under Article II, Section 1 of the Constitution *"to take care that the laws be faithfully executed,"* has directed the united States' Border Patrol agents to disregard the law.

President Trump directed to Border Patrol representatives to disobey United States existing law for not permitting refuges and migrants into the United States when visiting Calexico and California. The President also has given the direction to the Border Patrol groups saying misleading information to a judge "Sorry, judge, I can't do it. We don't have the room' whenever accused of disregarding the law. But after backing president from visiting, Border Patrol authorities further directed their agents that, in spite of the President's guidelines, they were obliged to comply with the law.

President *Donald J. Trump* has done several misuses of laws contradictory to their trust and belief as a President. To give direction to disobey the law to any authorities is subversive to the governmental general functioning and to make misunderstanding in the highest post of the powerful states, to weaken law and justice and to show the clear perverse of the people of the

United States.

Wherefore, the 45th President of the United States *Donald J. Trump* is guilty of an impeachable offense for removal from his office for instruction to border patrol to violate the law.

20. Refusal to Comply with Subpoenas

For determining the twentieth Article of Impeachment of the President of the United States, *Donald J. Trump*, it is selected to specify the issue of **'Refusal to Comply with Subpoenas'**, as an impeachable offense of the President *Donald J. Trump* because he personally and officially failed to produce witnesses, papers, and things as directed by duly authorized summonses which is completely contrary to the United States Constitutional responsibility under Article II, Section 1 of the Constitution *"to take care that the laws be faithfully executed."*

The President of the United States *Donald J. Trump* has failed without legitimate reason to present witnesses, evidential documents and things as directed by properly approved summonses issued by the Committee on the Judiciary of the House of Representatives on April 22, 2019. He also failed without any legitimate reason to present witnesses, evidential papers and things as issued by the Committee on Oversight and Government Reform of the

House of Representatives on April 2, 2019. The summoned witnesses, documents, and things were considered essential by the Committees for resolving and determining by direct basic proof, real issues identifying with Presidential direction, information, or endorsement of activities showed by other proof to be potential justification for impeachment of the President in the perspective of 'Russiagate'.

In declining to provide these witnesses, evidential documents, and evidential things *Donald J. Trump*, substituting his judgment concerning what materials were important for the investigations, interrupted the authorities of the Presidency against the legitimate summonses of the House of Representatives, in this manner accepting to himself capacities and decisions important to the implementation of the sole authority of impeachment conferred by the Constitution in the House of Representatives.

President *Donald J. Trump* has done numerous misuses of laws contradictory to their trust and belief as a President. To refuse to observe providing essential witnesses and documents to the lawful authorities is subversive to the governmental general functioning and to make misapprehension in the highest post of the powerful states, to weaken law and justice and to show the clear perverse of the people of the United States.

Wherefore, the 45th President of the United States *Donald J. Trump* is guilty of an impeachable offense for removal from his office for failing to present witnesses, evidential documents and things as directed by properly approved summonses issued legal bodies.

21. Declaration of Emergency Violating the Will of Congress without Basis

For determining the twenty first Article of Impeachment of the President of the United States, *Donald J. Trump*, it is selected to specify the issue of **'Affirmation of Emergency without Basis in Order to Violate the Will of Congress'**, as an impeachable offense of the President *Donald J. Trump* because he personally and officially violates the will of Congress to declare a state emergency without any basis which is completely contrary to the United States Constitutional responsibility under Article II, Section 1 of the Constitution *"to take care that the laws be faithfully executed."*

He, as the Chief Officer of the United States, has announced a state of emergency without any genuine crisis abusing the desire of Congress and give violent arms to Saudi Arabia for use in its ambush on non-military citizens in Yemen.

Another significant notorious example of his activity proves that he enjoyed the power exercising declaring state of emergency illegally by mitigating Iranian aggression including threatening attacks on Iran moving soldiers and weapons to the area, proclaiming some portion of the Iranian army to be a terrorist association, creating charges against Iran broadly questioned even by U.S. authorities, and - undoubtedly - giving weapons to Saudi Arabia.

Congress of the United Nations had been obstructing the deal of certain arms to Saudi Arabia, and the strong objective of the President *Donald J. Trump* behind announcing a national emergency by showing bogus crisis was to undermine the desire of Congress.

President *Donald J. Trump* has done numerous misuses of laws contradictory to their trust and belief as a President. To declare bogus emergency refusing the will of Congress is subversive to the governmental general functioning and to make misapprehension in the highest post of the powerful states, to weaken law and justice and to show the clear perverse of the people of the United States.

Wherefore, the 45th President of the United States *Donald J. Trump* is guilty of an impeachable offense for removal from his office for violating the will of congress by declaration of emergency without basis.

22. Unlawful Proliferation of Nuclear Technology

For determining the twenty second Article of Impeachment of the President of the United States, *Donald J. Trump*, it is selected to specify the issue of **'Illegal Proliferation of Nuclear Technology'**, as an impeachable offense of the President *Donald J. Trump* because his personal behavior and unlawful proliferation of nuclear technology which is completely contrary to the United States Constitutional responsibility under Article II, Section 1 of the Constitution *"to take care that the laws be faithfully executed,"* has questioned to unlawfully handover atomic technology to the administration of Saudi Arabia.

Section 123 of the United States Atomic Energy Act (AEA) of 1954 sets up the essentials prerequisites and procedures for major atomic alliance between the United States and other nations. A set of nine nonproliferation criteria must be fulfilled if any nation to go into such an accord with the United States. The United States has 26 bilateral nuclear cooperation agreements with 49 nations, *the International Atomic Energy Agency (IAEA)* and Taiwan with fulfilling nine nonproliferation criteria since January, 2019.

Authorization of Congress is obligatory to move atomic technology to any foreign nation. But Congress has not given its endorsement to such transfers atomic technology to Saudi Arabia, which has not focused on keeping away from exercises connected to a set of nine nonproliferation criteria.

However, by doing such agreement with Saudi Arabia without the approval of Congress, President *Donald J. Trump* has openly taken steps to generate atomic weapons. President *Donald J. Trump* has attempted endeavors for the benefit of the individuals who might benefit monetarily to move atomic innovation to Saudi Arabia. And President *Donald J. Trump* has totally declined to collaborate with the Congressional Committee analysis and examination of this issue, and not delivered a solo record demanded by the Congressional Committee.

President *Donald J. Trump* has committed numerous misuses of laws contradictory to their trust and belief as a President. To make illegal transfer atomic weapons technology to Saudi Arabia without taking permission from Congress is subversive to the governmental general functioning and violation of section 123 of the United States Atomic Energy Act (AEA) of 1954 and also to make misapprehension in the highest post of the powerful states, to weaken law and justice and to show the clear perverse of the people of the United States.

Wherefore, the 45th President of the United States *Donald J. Trump* is guilty of an impeachable offense for removal from his office for violating section 123 of the United States Atomic Energy Act (AEA) of 1954 and ignoring Congress's authority by illegal proliferation of nuclear technology.

23. Illegitimately Eliminating the United States from the Intermediate-Range Nuclear Forces Treaty

For determining the twenty third Article of Impeachment of the President of the United States, *Donald J. Trump*, it is selected to specify the issue of **'*Illegitimately Eliminating the United States from the Intermediate-Range Nuclear Forces Treaty*',** as an impeachable offense of the President *Donald J. Trump* because his personal behavior and illegitimately removing the United States from the intermediate-range nuclear forces treaty which is completely contrary to the United States Constitutional responsibility under Article II, Section 1 of the Constitution *"to take care that the laws be faithfully executed."* Donald J. Trump has unlawfully removing the United States from *the Intermediate-Range Nuclear Forces (INF) Treaty* in violation of his constitutional oath to authentically accomplish the office of President of the United States.

Article VI, Clause 2 of the United States Constitution states that

> *"This Constitution, and the Laws of the United States which shall be made in Pursuance thereof; and all Treaties made, or which shall be made, under the Authority of the United States, shall be the supreme Law of the Land; and the Judges in every State shall be bound thereby, any Thing in the Constitution or Laws of any State to the Contrary notwithstanding."*

According to Article VI, Clause 2 of the United States Constitution, *the Intermediate-Range Nuclear Forces (INF) Treaty* becoming the supreme law of the land when *the Intermediate-Range Nuclear Forces (INF) Treaty* was approved by signing President Reagan on December 8, 1987, and approved by assent of the U.S. Senate on May 27, 1988.

The Intermediate-Range Nuclear Forces (INF) Treaty permits withdrawal of the United States as a party of the INF Treaty only if exceptional occasions identified with the topic of this INF Treaty have endangered its supreme advantages.

President *Donald J. Trump* has committed

numerous misuses of laws contradictory to their trust and belief as a President. To make illegal withdrawing from *the Intermediate-Range Nuclear Forces (INF) Treaty* is subversive to the governmental general functioning and violation of constitutional supreme functioning and also to make misapprehension in the highest post of the powerful states, to weaken law and justice and to show the clear perverse of the people of the United States.

Wherefore, the 45th President of the United States *Donald J. Trump* is guilty of an impeachable offense for removal from his office for violation of Article VI, Clause 2 of the United States Constitution by illegally withdrawing from *the Intermediate-Range Nuclear Forces (INF) Treaty*.

24. Pursuing to Utilize Foreign Governments to Investigate Against Political Rivals

For determining the twenty fourth Article of Impeachment of the President of the United States, *Donald J. Trump*, it is selected to specify the issue of **'Pursuing to Utilize Foreign Governments to Investigate Against Political Rivals',** as an impeachable offense of the President *Donald J. Trump* because his personal behavior and illegitimate pressuring Ukrainian President *Volodymyr Zelenskiy* to investigate political opponent the U.S. former Vice President Joe Biden and his son Hunter Biden which is completely contrary to the United States Constitutional responsibility under Article II, Section 1 of the Constitution *"to take care that the laws be faithfully executed."*

Donald J. Trump has tried to influence Ukrainian President *Volodymyr Zelenskiy* to inquiry alleged activities of Democratic Party opponents including presidential competitor Joseph Biden and his son Robert Hunter Biden. President Trump may have been intimidating to hold back the funding for weapons that had been allocate by the U.S. Congress from Ukraine at the same time he was influencing its new president *Volodymyr Zelenskiy* to investigate against political rival Joe Biden and his son.

Only one week before of talking telephone by the President Trump with newly elected President *Volodymyr Zelenskiy* in Ukrainian in late July, he directed his acting head of staff, *Mick Mulvaney*, to put off on discharging about $400 million in military assistance for Ukraine that had just been allocated by Congress of the United States.

Regardless of this open grasp of his activities, President Trump freely recommended that whoever had made the material of his call with

President *Volodymyr Zelenskiy* known ought to be murdered.

President *Donald J. Trump* has committed numerous misuses of laws contradictory to their trust and belief as a President. By threatening for withdrawing military aid from Ukraine President for not doing investigation of political rivals is subversive to the governmental general functioning and violation of constitutional supreme functioning and also to make misapprehension in the highest post of the powerful states, to weaken law and justice and to show the clear perverse of the people of the United States.

Wherefore, the 45th President of the United States *Donald J. Trump* is guilty of an impeachable offense for removal from his office for violation of Federal Law (52 U.S. Code § 30121. Contributions and donations by foreign nationals) of the United States by unlawfully threatening for withdrawing military aid from any foreign country.

25. Refusal to Comply with Impeachment Inquiry

For determining the twenty fifth Article of Impeachment of the President of the United States, *Donald J. Trump*, it is selected to specify the issue of **'Refusal to Comply with**

Impeachment Inquiry', as an impeachable offense of the President *Donald J. Trump* because his personal behavior and not to complying with impeachment investigation which is completely contrary to the United States Constitutional responsibility under Article II, Section 1 of the Constitution *"to take care that the laws be faithfully executed."*

Donald J. Trump has declined to conform with summonses issued by Congress as a component of an investigation of impeachment.

The Judiciary Committee of the House of Representatives accepted an article of impeachment against then-President Richard M. Nixon blaming him for overlooking to conform to Congressional subpoenas on July 27, 1974. The President of the United States *Donald J. Trump* has comparatively would not agree to subpoenas. So, the Judiciary Committee of the House of Representatives should accept an article of impeachment against then-President *Donald J. Trump* accusing him for overlooking to conform to Congressional subpoenas

President *Donald J. Trump* has committed numerous misappropriations of laws contrary to their trust and belief as a President. By refusing to comply with impeachment investigation is subversive to the governmental general functioning and violation of constitutional supreme functioning and also to make misapprehension in the highest post of the powerful states, to weaken law and justice and to show the clear perverse of the people of the United States.

Wherefore, the 45th President of the United States *Donald J. Trump* is guilty of an impeachable offense for removal from his office for not complying with the refusing to follow to Congressional subpoenas.

26. Threatening To Dismantle The Proposition That No Person Is Above The Law

For determining the twenty sixth Article of Impeachment of the President of the United States, *Donald J. Trump*, it is selected to specify the issue of **'Threatening To Dismantle The Proposition That No Person Is Above The Law',** as an impeachable offense of the President *Donald J. Trump* because his personal behavior and various statements is completely contrary to the United States Constitutional responsibility under Article II, Section 1 of the Constitution *"to take care that the laws be faithfully executed."*

By openly and constantly violating the United States' constitutional standards and by layering disruptive action upon disruptive action,

President Trump has endangered to disassemble the conception of rule of law that no person is above the law.

President *Donald J. Trump* has committed numerous misappropriations of laws contrary to their trust and belief as a President. By threatening to dismantle the proposition that no person is above the law which is actual subversive to the governmental general functioning and violation of constitutional supreme functioning and also to make misapprehension in the highest post of the powerful states, to weaken law and justice and to show the clear perverse of the people of the United States.

Wherefore, the 45th President of the United States *Donald J. Trump* is guilty of an impeachable offense for removal from his office for threatening to dismantle the proposition that no person is above the law.

CHAPTER SIX

TRUMP IMPEACHMENT: POSSIBILITY-IMPOSSIBILITY

Is it really possible to overthrow President Trump?

The hearing for the impeachment of the United States President Trump has begun.

Now, examination and re-examination of witness, hearings and inquiries are started before the Congress Committee. This is a public process and the American people are watching daily on the TV screen with all over the people.

Charges against *Donald Trump* is that he pressurized Ukrainian President *Zelenskiy* as he investigated allegations of corruption against former US Vice President Joe Biden and his son Hunter Biden - that Mr. Biden is the Democrat President candidate competing with *Donald Trump* as in the next presidential election.

Democrat Congress members has been launched officially investigation to prosecute *Donald Trump*.

Will this process succeed? To get the answer to this question, you need to read the every page of this book where it is discussed how the process works.

The impeachment procedure is a very difficult and rare process in the U.S. constitutional history. Impeachment means that a person holding a government federal office is accused of misconduct in Congress.

The US constitution is described in using few words about to impeach an American president, but the task is not easy.

First, a charge of misconduct or delinquency against the president should bring in the House of Representatives of the US Congress, followed by a judicial process in the Senate.

It's a process that is quite difficult and rare.

After the hearing in the House of Representatives of Congress, the general majority is enough to pass the article of the impeachment, with a total of 218 votes to be casted in favor of the article of the impeachment.

But convicting Trump and removing him from the post of President, the Senate would require a two-thirds majority, that is, the support of at least sixty seven senators.

It is thought to be less likely to happen of impeachment.

Because, there are forty seven Republican senators supporting Trump in the present Senate. As a result, it seems unlikely that sixty seven votes will be received in the Senate for impeachment.

So what has happened in the past?

The presidential impeachment has been happened twice in U.S. history by impeachment of two presidents, Andrew Johnson in 1868 and Bill Clinton in 1998.

However, they did not have to step down from their post. Both were acquitted during the Senate trial. However, President Richard Nixon resigned before the Impeachment due to the Watergate scandal.

So, it is crystal clear that if the article of impeachment to impeach President *Donald Trump* is passed in the House of Representatives, but not in the Senate.

Many federal officials including president have acquitted from impeachment by this Senate.

Currently, the Democrats have a majority in the House of Representatives of the US Congress, with 233 members. However, in the Senate, Republicans have 47 senators. Therefore, a two-thirds majority will not be able to impeach in the Senate trail unless the Republican Senators Vote for Trump's impeachment.

So why is this impeachment process happening at all?

The answer to this question is the reckoning of US pre-election politics.

There has been debate among his political opponents over whether to prosecute President Trump.

Democrats, who favor the prosecution, think a

formal investigation into the prosecution will be aimed at changing the American public. According to them, if the US public opinion is not in favor of it now, if the evidence against Trump is collected and presented vigorously, the public will support the Democrat in the next election.

Many Democrats feel that the impeachment is a moral obligation, because the president violated the law, and violated his oath and Constitutional responsibility. If not take action against the violation of the law and justice, it would mean giving indirect consent to it and encouraging the President to break more laws.

There has been debate in the Democrat camp about whether this will be an issue to win politically.

Some Democrats, including Speaker Nancy Pelosi, have expressed concern that impeachment could consolidate the backbone of Republicans, and may create frustration among moderates - because they want Congress to focus on policymakers.

The United States Constitutional history says, no matter how strong the accusation against Trump may be, literally, there is no real way to be effective it by impeachment of the President *Donald Trump*.

Because the Republicans still hold the majority in the Senate. But such propaganda against Trump before the presidential election at next year 2020 is certainly not a relief for him. In addition, the 'voice' of the impeachment procedure can disrupt the dream of becoming a second time president of the United States.

Can Trump Be Acquitted from the Impeachment prosecution?

The present U.S. President *Donald Trump* is now in power.

But the throne the U.S. President *Donald J. Trump* is now in crisis. The US Congress delegation can prosecute him (equivalent to the accused), the House of Representatives must impeach the President. It cannot be sworn that whether the Senate will vote to convict him and remove him from office. Trump's recent actions have prompted strong accusations of impeachment.

In particular, the pressure on the foreign government for its own political benefit (which could be considered a serious crime under the Federal Laws).

According to a document leaked by a CIA member to the U.S. Central Intelligence Agency, Trump spoke to Ukrainian President *Volodymyr*

Zelenskiy on the phone July 25, 2019. At that time, Trump pressurized the Ukrainian president to investigate allegations of corruption against his main rival, Democrat president candidate Joe Biden, in the 2012 elections. *Zelenskiy* mentions Ukraine's military needs. *Zelenskiy* told to Trump over phone that his country was interested in buying anti-tank missiles from the United States. Instead of saying 'yes' directly to Trump, he said, *"Let me do you a favor."* And that is you investigate Joe Biden's corruption. Trump ordered *Zelenskiy* to work with his personal lawyer, Rudolph Gilliani, and Attorney General William Barr to investigate Joe Biden's corruption.

Trump and his associates allege Joe Biden was forced to sack a Ukrainian lawyer to save his son Hunter Biden, who served as board director of a large gas company in Ukraine. However, the allegations were strongly rejected by Joe Biden's supporters. Nevertheless, Trump is putting pressure on a foreign state to investigate corruption against rivals to win elections like the 2016.

The transcript of Trump's conversation with *Zelenskiy* shocked readers of both teams at Capitol Hill. Trump rejected the advice of his aides and decided to release the transcript, because he thought it would release him from the charges. But now, it turns out that this transcript has turned him into an impeachment.

In the beginning, Speaker of the House of Representatives, Nancy Pelosi, was resisting the Democrats' call to launch an impeachment investigation against Trump. He feared that the impeachment process would threaten the Democrats' wining in the 2020 president election. He also thought that such efforts could have adverse consequences. That could increase Trump's support. But Nancy Pelosi changed now her mind. She said that the president must be held accountable. Because, he violated so many laws which is questioned the trust of his oath. He also violated the constitutional duty he had.

Although Trump has described himself as an 'extremely talented genius', the truth is that he now seems to be lopsided. Trump is now seeking the identity of the CIA member who leaked the details of his conversation with *Volodymyr Zelenskiy*, which could endanger that officer's life. He blames Adam Schiff, the chair of the House of Representatives' intelligence committee, for leaking this information. He has already announced that the traitors will be shot or hanged. I don't think such a threat to Trump will help him survive in power.

Speaker Nancy Pelosi has directed officials to

start an investigation into the matter. The investigation will verify what Trump said by calling the president of Ukraine and then decide whether he committed a *"high crime and misdemeanor"*. If a criminal offense is found, it will be voted in the House of Representatives after hearing. Democrats hold the majority in this House. As a result, it may pass very easily by the majority of the House. Then it will be sent to the Senate for trail. Here, a two-thirds majority is required to pass the impeachment trial. But the Senate controls the Republicans. Although there are many views on this, Republican members of Congress will vote against Trump — I never want to ruin this possibility. Because, they are too disappointed with Trump's actions and aggressive behavior. They think that Trump's actions are damaging to the party and that is why it is best to leave Trump. Few Republicans can support him. Now, let's see what happens to Trump's fate.

He could be the third?

President *Donald J. Trump* may be impeached and removed from the President in the 300 hundred years of American political history.

ABOUT THE AUTHOR

Zulfiquar Ahmed, **PhD**. Currently, he is an Associate Professor of Law at the University of Rajshahi specializing in Government, politics, Cyber and e-commerce law.

Dr. Zulfiquar Ahmed has written numerous academic articles on Government, internet and law. He has authored many books, like, *Government, Politics and Election Laws, Political Theory, A Hand Book of Computer & Law; A Text book of Bangladesh Labour Act 2006; A Text Book on Cyber Law in Bangladesh, Alternative Dispute Resolution*, etc. He is a columnist on different political issues including legal matters. He introduced 'Cyber Law' as a new course in Bangladesh to be offered in the Department of Law, University of Rajshahi. Dr. Ahmed is an architect of the Digital Security Law, 2018 in Bangladesh. He is also a legal consultant to Bangladesh government, professional organizations and business corporations.

www.ingramcontent.com/pod-product-compliance
Lightning Source LLC
Chambersburg PA
CBHW030624220526
45463CB00004B/1407